Angel Warrior

Sharon Luca

MARCIA M
PUBLISHING HOUSE

Angel Warrior

Authored by Sharon Luca

©copyright angel warrior 2020

Edited by Marcia M Publishing House Editorial Team Published by Marcia
M Spence of Marcia M Publishing House, West Bromwich, West Midlands the
UNITED KINGDOM B71

All rights reserved 2020 Marcia M Publishing House

MARCIA M
PUBLISHING HOUSE

www.marciampublishing.com

DEDICATION

To my husband Jas & son Ky for being the one's who keep me going. They literally are the one's I get out of bed for each morning since losing Luca and then the chronic pain of Fibromyalgia. They are my rocks & reason for living.

ACKNOWLEDGMENTS

Many thanks to Shelley Wilson Writing Solutions for her guidance and roadmap on how to write this book. As my first book I most certainly needed this guidance.

To Marcia M Publishing House for supporting my timescale to have this available for Baby loss awareness week October 2020.

All my close family and friends who have supported me on this hard journey so far...they know who they are! Their understanding when I cancel plans late in the day due to fatigue & pain that will not pass. Their continued support & love on Luca's birthday each year, it means so much to us knowing they have not forgotten our first son.

And finally the Lord himself, whose given me the strength to keep going & made my faith stronger. Coventry Cathedral has become my place of inner peace and played a huge part in this journey to date. The place where my prayers are answers and ideas have come to me.

Donations & support;

10% of the profits from this book will support the work of The Luca Foundation www.thelucafoundation.org.uk where you can also purchase 'Why did Grandad Die'. That book supports the mental health of children when explaining bereavement & all profits from that go to the Charity.

You can purchase your 'Angel Warrior' top from LK Eco Style www.lkecostyle.com

With code AW25 all bereaved parents (new name 'Angel Warrior') will receive 25% off their purchase of the 'Angel Warrior' range of clothing & accessories.

Together we will all make society understand this new name 'Angel Warrior', means bereaved parent!

Follow The Luca Foundation at;

Instagram: @thelucafoundation

Twitter: @foundationluca

Facebook page: The Luca Foundation

Follow LK Eco Style at;

Instagram: @lk_eco_style

Twitter: @eco_lk

Facebook page: LK Eco Style

Soon to some LK Media, follow LK Eco Style for more details on that. This is where we will invite more parents to open up about their journey & help others through theirs. If this is something you would like to be part of, please email.

INTRODUCTION

Before I met Jas, my future husband, there was a lot of planning behind the scenes to get us together. My cousin and another distant family member who played football with Jas thought we would make the perfect couple. So, they spoke to us both and we agreed to exchange email addresses.

The first time Jas emailed me I could sense the nervousness in his wording. It was quite cute. We did a little bit of general chit-chat, just to get to know the basics of each other really. Then I thought: well, I'm going to lay everything on the line, be upfront and honest because I didn't want to waste his time.

Jas is Indian and a Sikh, so I explained that I was not your average Indian; I'm Christian by faith and my family are a mix of cultures. I told him that I had been married, but was a victim of domestic abuse, so was now divorced. I said if any of this was a problem for him, he should tell me right away. He thanked me for being honest and told me he thought honesty and trust were key in starting any relationship. He assured me that what I'd told him about my past wasn't a problem for him and that we all had history. He also explained that he hadn't been married, but had been in a committed relationship, which came to an end a couple of years before. I asked if he thought his family would have an issue with anything I had told him. He was adamant that if down the line, we chose to be together, it didn't matter what the family said; it was about what made us happy. This was quite a relief to me, as my ex-husband had been quite the opposite — wanting approval from family members, and doing anything to get it, rather than making sure I was happy. Of course, I hadn't known this until I'd entered

1

into the marriage, which had been arranged quickly. Thankfully, there's never been an arranged marriage in my family since. In fact, we've all been free to marry whoever we wanted. The family definitely learnt a lot from that disastrous marriage.

After a couple of weeks of emailing, Jas suggested we meet, and I only agreed to this because I was close to my cousin and didn't want to disappoint her. But I wasn't really expecting much to come of this. I'd been on other blind dates, which were awful, so I always made sure I had a backup call planned: where a friend would call me half an hour into my meeting with the blind date, just in case I didn't like the guy and then I'd have an excuse for a quick getaway.

We decided to meet on a Saturday for drinks. Unfortunately, I had to rearrange because I came down with an awful cold. I was in bed for three days and off work. Although Jas decided to play golf with his friends, he did text me a few times over that weekend to find out how I was feeling. I thought how sweet and caring he was and felt quite comforted by that.

When eventually we did meet at a bar, there was certainly a physical attraction, because Jas is so good looking. But the main thing was, we were really comfortable talking to one another. It was as if we'd known each other a while, but of course we had been talking by email and text quite a lot, which had broken the ice. We talked about football - he is an Everton supporter and I'm an Arsenal fan. It was during the 2008 Euros, so we discussed the teams who were favorites to win the competition. A couple of hours went by so quickly and we departed on a good note, neither of us actually saying that we would meet up again. I suppose for me I just wanted to hear it from him; but because Jas is quite shy, he prefers to do things by text.

Well, he did text and we arranged to meet again. I hadn't realised, however, that the night we had arranged to meet was when Spain were playing in the Euros, so I actually rearranged our date by text. In his reply, he asked me if everything was okay and I said: "Yes, but I just didn't realise when we set the date that Spain were playing that night, and I want to watch the match." He sent me a message saying: "L.O.L! I can't believe I've actually met a woman who would cancel a date for a football match! It's flipping fantastic!"

During the first few weeks I was dating Jas, an aunt of mine had called my mother saying that at her son's wedding, which was coming up, she'd like to introduce me to her husband's nephew. At this point my mum didn't know that I was seeing Jas. I hadn't told her, as I was still getting to know him, but the idea of meeting somebody else just turned my stomach. I realised at that point that I did really like Jas and that we had a good connection. Nonetheless, I went along with it knowing that I wouldn't be interested. As soon as the 'potential mate' was pointed out to me at the wedding, I just said 'no' and left it at that.

After I'd been seeing Jas for a couple of months, and knowing that I really liked him, and the feeling was mutual, I decided I wanted him to meet my brothers. It had to be within a certain time-frame, because my brother, Sunny, was in the Royal Marines and was on leave, and Steven had come back from London to spend a week at home in the Midlands. Jas agreed and we all met at a bar. He was so quiet compared to the Jas I knew. The three guys did talk a little about football as there was a match playing at the time on the TV in the background. When Jas went to the restroom, my brothers laughed and asked if he ever spoke. I explained that he was probably nervous around them and that he wasn't normally like that at all. Well, it turned out I was right. Jas told me later that he felt nervous and shy and didn't know what to say. Now, after we've been together for twelve years, he's well and truly 'one of the lads' with my brothers.

A couple of weeks later we decided to take our first holiday together - a few days in Barcelona. It was fantastic and was a time to really open up and get to know each other even more. We went to the Camp Nou Stadium, which we both enjoyed even though I had been there before with my cousin Karen. We had a great time looking around, eating, taking photos. We were both so interested in the same things. It was fantastic! Now I knew he was the one. We came back refreshed and got stuck back into work. I was a Business Development Manager; I wasn't having the greatest time at work as there were a lot of changes going on and I was a bit stressed about it all.

A month after our holiday in Barcelona, Jas suggested we go away for a few days again, to get my mind off it all. I agreed I needed a break. At this point my parents were away on holiday, so I suggested he come and stay with me so that he could get to know my German Shepherd, Kane. He was a big dog and was quite intimidating; but when Kane liked someone, he was soft. Kane was my baby and if Jas had not liked him, it would have been a deal-breaker. In my head, I had already imagined that if Jas and I got married, Kane would come to live with us. So, I gently introduced him to Jas. I could see that he already adored Kane, and to my great relief, the feeling was mutual. We booked our holiday to Fuerteventura in the Canary Islands for early November. In our household we always took it in turns to take our holidays so that there was always someone at home for Kane. He officially belonged to my brothers and I, but my parents were just as attached to him, and they were always happy to take care of him.

It was beautifully warm on our holiday. Even though I generally like it a bit hotter it was still nice to be away with Jas. We went to a bar on some days to watch the football, walked around and explored the area on other days, and then lay by the pool and just chilled. One evening, we were at a restaurant and had both had a couple of drinks. We were talking about his friend who was getting married, and because I was a bit tipsy, which made me bold, I asked Jas what he thought about marriage. He said that if he was with the right person, he would definitely get married. I asked, cheekily: "Have you met the right person yet?" He smiled and said: "I love you." This was the first time he'd said those three little words. Then he said: "And 'yes' you're the right person, Sharon." I was overjoyed. "That's good, because I love you too, Jas!" Then we hugged and kissed. It was such a beautiful moment. "Now I guess we should tell our families," I said.

Jas was going to drop me off at home when we got back to England, so I suggested that perhaps he could meet my parents then. He was quite okay with that, so I texted my mum and told her what time we'd be back and that I'd like her and dad to meet Jas. She was delighted that finally they were going to get to meet him. Mum had made dinner and chatted with Jas to find out about him and his family. Kane was walking around showing that he was extremely comfortable with Jas, but then came to have cuddles with me, as we always missed each other when I was away. My dad came home shortly after and also had a good conversation with Jas. After Jas had left, they both told me that they really liked him, and I was glad.

Now it was time for Jas to tell his family. He said he would talk to his mum first since she knew he was seeing somebody, although he'd never given her any details. She was surprised and pleased when he told her he wanted to marry me, but obviously wanted to know more. He told her a few things about me and then went to tell his dad. His dad was really happy and wanted to see a photo of me. Jas laughed. He knew why - a family member had married someone who didn't quite meet the family's expectations in the looks department. He texted me and asked me to send some photos for his dad to see. I laughed too and sent him photos. His dad said he was pleased with what he saw and asked when they would get to meet me. We arranged for us all to meet at his family home In Coventry. I was so nervous, I really didn't know what to expect, but luckily it went really well.

It was my cousin's twenty-first birthday party the following week and I knew my grandad would be there. I decided to tell him that I had met Jas and we wanted to get married. He was delighted and surprised, as he always thought I would marry a British white man. He asked if I was sure I wanted to marry an Indian British guy. I laughed and told him that I did because he was a nice guy and like me was 'a coconut' – brown on the outside and white on the inside. A common joke in our family.

When I first started talking to Jas, I was really surprised to find out that we were both born on the same day – 16 March. What are the chances of that? Well, in March the following year we went to Egypt for a holiday to celebrate. The pyramids were amazing, of course, and the camels too. It was so different from anywhere else we'd visited. It was also hot, just the way I like it, and one day we decided to take a trip into the desert and mountains on quad bikes. It was so much fun. We stopped at the bottom of a hilltop and had a drink before going up the hill. We went quite high up and could see so much of the country and the desert. It was very peaceful. We took some photos and then Jas bent down on one knee and I thought he was going to do up his shoelace, but it was right there and then that he proposed to me. I was delighted. He didn't have a ring because he had no idea what kind of ring to get me, and thought it better that I choose one myself, which I was happy with. I was very glad to have had such a romantic and memorable proposal in a beautiful and exotic country.

Now we were officially engaged, we went to the Jewellery Quarter in Birmingham so that I could pick out an engagement ring. My fingers are quite small, so I had to have one made specially, which was great because I got to design it myself. I chose a beautiful one-carat cushion-cut diamond, sitting on a crown of small diamonds with diamonds down the neck of the ring. It was perfect.

We had quite a small formal engagement party at my parent's home. Jas's family came and met my family. It was then that my dad and uncle realised that they used to play football with Jas's uncles back in the 1970s. Small world, hey? They were all laughing and reminiscing about the olden days. My grandad was so happy, it wasn't very often that you would see him merry, but on this occasion, he was, and beaming with pride.

Whilst I was in Egypt, my dad had noticed that something wasn't quite right with Kane. When I came back, he said he thought Kane needed to go the vet as he'd got a lump on his throat. I felt around his throat area and there was a small lump there. The vet detected something and said that she would need to keep Kane in for a day to do some tests. He didn't really like going to the vet, so it was a bit of a mission to leave him there. It was almost like settling a baby at nursery. I had to stay with him until he was comfortable.

I got a call in the afternoon and the vet confirmed that Kane had lymphoma. I was devastated when I took the call and realised that we wouldn't have him for long. My mum and I sobbed, and I suggested we got our tears out then before he came home. I didn't want him to see our tears. When I went to the vet to pick him up, he ran out with joy and jumped up at me to lick my face. I could tell he had missed me and was happy to see me, just as I was to see my beloved Kane. He was put on steroid medication and something else to keep him going. They couldn't put a time limit on the length of his life but said if he took well to the medication, he could continue to have a good life. This was very reassuring, so we went home, and I made him some of his favourite food.

A couple of weeks after the engagement party, my parents had planned to go to Turkey on holiday. The day they were due to leave, Kane was in a bad way and could hardly move. My mum woke me up and told me and I rushed downstairs to Kane. I could see in his face that he was defeated, and I decided this was it. I called my brothers and asked them to come home and say their goodbyes to Kane, because the time had come for him to go. Sunny was down at the Marine base and Steven was in London. He was able to come home easily, but with Sunny being in the Marines we weren't sure whether he would be able to get back. He was relieved when his General said he understood the importance of the situation, as he was a dog owner himself, and he allowed Sunny to take leave.

My parents left for Turkey that afternoon, and because they knew Kane wouldn't be there on their return, they sobbed as they left the house. I cried as well as I said goodbye to them, knowing what was to come. My mum had called my aunt to come over to support me through this ordeal. My uncle and aunt arrived about an hour before Sunny and Steven. I had called Jas in the afternoon to explain what was happening. He played football on Saturdays, so he hadn't heard my messages. When he did call back and I was crying, he said he'd come over immediately. Sunny's girlfriend Olivia was there too, as well as Steven's girlfriend, Grace. It was a chance for everyone to say their goodbyes to Kane.

I had called the vet that afternoon and asked her to come to the house, I didn't want to leave Kane suffering. Inside I knew that if anyone was going to lift Kane's mood, it would be my brothers. He saw Sunny as his master, Steven his buddy who played games with him, and I was his carer. Sunny and Steven arrived quite soon after each other. Steven was first but there wasn't really a change in Kane's mood, although he had moved his position slightly when he saw Steven. When Sunny came in the door, Kane walked a few steps towards him and then lay down again. It was clear to us all that he had had enough. I had decided when the vet arrived that only Sunny, Steven and I would be with Kane for his last moments.

About an hour or so later the vet who had seen Kane arrived. My brothers and I sat on the floor next to Kane stroking him, kissing his nose, and acting as though everything was fine. The last thing we wanted was for Kane to feel nervous or anxious in his last moments. I was whispering to him: "Good boy...well done...good boy," while the vet administered the needle. My lovely dog was looking at me, and then suddenly, he was gone. The three of us rested our foreheads on Kane's lifeless body and cried our eyes out. It was the most horrible feeling - losing our beloved dog who'd been with our family for eight years.

Everyone came out from the lounge when they heard us crying, and my uncle took me in his arms. I snuggled on his shoulder and then my Jas came in and he held me. I couldn't stop crying. Grace was comforting Steven and Sunny was comforted by Olivia. After a short while the vet said we needed to take him to the car, and she gave us a blanket to put underneath him. As I said before, he was a large dog, around nine stone, so it took the strength of both Sunny and Steven to pick him up. It was the last time I'd ever see him or touch him or say hello. He belonged to all three of us as we all lived at home together when we first got him, so we all carried him out for this final time, sobbing our hearts out.

When my parents came back from their holiday they walked in and cried as there was now no Kane to greet any of us. There was certainly a big void in the house without him. After a few weeks, my mum said she couldn't stand the emptiness and that she wanted to get another dog. I suggested we waited a little longer although I had been feeling the same too. When Sunny came back on leave we discussed the idea and he said he was heartbroken too, but he didn't think another dog was going to help. Mum was adamant she wanted another dog. I was fifty-fifty. Mum saw an advert about pedigree German Shepherds for sale near Birmingham. Sunny agreed to go and have a look but commented that another dog was not going to be another Kane. Mum acknowledged that two dogs can't be the same, just as two people aren't alike.

So mum, Sunny, Olivia and I went off to see the litter of puppies. Well, I bet you know what happened here. We all fell in love with a cute little German Shepherd puppy with a bit of red colouring. He seemed like the most well-behaved puppy out of the whole litter. We knew we wanted a male dog, and since he was the one we all felt most comfortable with, we put a deposit down for him there and then, knowing that we would collect him in about three weeks. My mum asked me to pick a name for him. Sunny and I laughed about the way the three of us (Sunny, Steven & I) had chosen Kane's name. You see all three of us had been big wrestling fans in the early 2000s. I wanted 'The Rock' as he was my favourite wrestler. We were going through the list of all the names of wrestlers we could think of, but none seemed right. Then, almost simultaneously, we all looked at each other and said "Kane!" and that was the one that stuck.

My mum's favourite film was 'Troy' or at least one of her favourites, and she loved that name. So, as this new German Shepherd was going to be hers and my dad's, although he was quite annoyed that we were getting another dog so soon, Mum picked the name Troy. I called Anne, the breeder, and asked her to start calling the dog, Troy, so that he got used it. She loved the name.

A few weeks later, Troy was with us in our big family home. He was certainly no Kane - he was a little devil, with more energy than he had shown on the day we went to see him. My goodness, he was hard work as a puppy but so cute at the same time. It was June 2009 by now.

The following month my grandad decided he wanted to go to India with his sons. My dad has three brothers and two of them were to go with him. They were all looking forward to it. I dropped my dad off at the airport in Birmingham and then went to see my grandad to wish him a good holiday and give him a big hug. There was something different about my grandad that day. He was overjoyed to be going, but also talking in a way that suggested he wasn't coming back. Then he used a phrase, something like: "If I come back." I said: "What do you mean if?" and he laughed.

Whilst having a good time in the family village in India, one evening my grandad collapsed. He died quite quickly in my dad's arms. We were all devastated when we heard the news. I couldn't believe it. My grandad had gone. He was eighty-three. The funeral took place within the week, in India. Two of my aunts and cousins went from here as it was within days that a cremation would take place

By the end of October, I had planned to go to India with my mum, my grandma, and my cousin to Punjab to do my wedding shopping. We visited my Grandad's estate, but it didn't feel the same without him there, it made me cry. I had designed my own wedding outfit and wanted to have it made In India. I also wanted to purchase gifts of clothing for my new in-laws. I was delighted my mum's cousin was there as well. It was great fun staying at her house and taking her shopping with us. It was lovely to see my mum's relatives who hadn't seen her for many years and to hear childhood stories about my mum. The shopping was a success and we were back home after two weeks. Jas and I stayed in contact via our mobile phones. I couldn't wait to get back to see him; I missed him so much.

Jas and I had already started looking for a house before I had gone away, and he'd continued searching and had compiled a list of houses we could go and see. We soon found one that we really loved. It was a four-bedroomed detached home that was not too far from my family - sort of in the middle really, between both families. We put in an offer on the house, which was accepted, and we were excited about getting things moving.

By the new year, we were in a good place - all the searches had been done, and we were getting ready to exchange contracts. This was a very exciting time for us. We planned to do so much to the house to make it our own and knew that we would be able to get started prior to the wedding. Approximately ten days before we were due to sign the papers, however, the sellers decided to back out. I was crushed. We'd been so excited as we knew this would be a lovely home for us, and we'd already ordered furniture. The sellers had backed out because the gentleman was poorly, but we were still so upset and even had to pay the solicitor's fees for all the work he'd done.

We were now desperately trying to find a home. We started looking again and by March, three weeks before our wedding, we found a house that we really liked in Warwickshire. We put in an offer that evening and after a couple of calls, we negotiated a price that was agreed. We urged the solicitor to hurry things along. It was a vacant property so all we were waiting for were the searches, as our mortgage was already in place. Things developed quickly, and five days before our wedding we signed and exchanged contracts. It had been quite a manic time, but we were relieved, nonetheless.

It was now April and our wedding was due to take place in a few days. Snow had been forecast, so we were panicking a little. I do like to be in control of things, but you can't control the weather. Overall, everything was fine, and I was on a high as I was going to marry my soulmate.

The wedding was on a Sunday, Easter Sunday actually, symbolic for me as a Christian starting a new life. On the Friday before - Good Friday - we had a henna party at my mum's house. Because I'm a Christian I didn't really want a Sikh wedding. However, as it was Jas's first wedding, I obliged. I couldn't take that away from him. Planning everything had been so much fun, and the wedding would be just as I'd wanted it to be. Saturday was my pre-wedding party, in a school hall near my parents' home, in fact the Primary school we all attended as children., and everyone had a good time dancing.

Then it was the big day. I felt nervous, but in a good way. Jas texted me that morning, around 6 a.m. He said: "I love you, my baby. Today you will be all mine." It was a beautiful message and put a massive smile on my face as I was getting ready.

Our wedding day went perfectly. Luckily, it didn't snow, and even though it was cold, the sun was shining. We had a great day with all of our friends and family. It meant so much to us that they were all there, but I did miss my grandad because he had been looking forward to my wedding day. My new husband and I spent the night in a hotel, along with a bottle of champagne.

It is traditional, the day after the wedding, for the bride to go back to her parents' home with her new husband for dinner. So, my entire family: uncles, aunts, and cousins, gathered at my mum and dad's house to eat and talk about our fabulous wedding day. It was another big party and loads of fun.

The following morning, we went off to our honeymoon in South Africa. We had the best honeymoon, seeing Cape Town, going on safari and to Mauritius. In between the safari and Mauritius, we went to Johannesburg where I had arranged for us to play with lion cubs, something I had always wanted to do. I am very fond of the big cats and this experience was absolutely amazing.

Reality hit when we got back to England. So much needed doing to the house, jobs that we didn't realise at the time of purchase. We'd thought it would be a simple decorating exercise, but no, it all needed gutting and re-plastering. We spent four months renovating the house, putting in a new kitchen, a bathroom - pretty much everything was new. But it was now the way we wanted it. So that was nice. Not the ideal start to marriage that we had hoped for, but nonetheless we made the best of it and finally moved into our little haven. It was just the two of us making plans for our future, and the next big chapter in our lives would be: starting a family. We said we would wait a year before we started trying so that we could save up to have our first baby.

Chapter One
Stolen Time

The following year in October 2011, it was just amazing to see the test which said I was two to three weeks pregnant. We were so overjoyed and emotional as we had wanted this so much. We felt everything we wanted was coming together. I was really well in the pregnancy and barely had any morning sickness. I loved being pregnant, loved my bump growing and really embraced it all.

We debated whether we wanted to know the gender of the baby, but Jas said he wasn't sure he could keep it to himself therefore, I knew he couldn't be trusted to find out. I knew I could keep it to myself however so, at our twenty-week scan I put a note in with my maternity notes and asked for the gender of the baby to be written down. I was delighted to find out we were having a boy as I knew Jas had always wanted a boy first. I wasn't actually bothered whether it was a boy or a girl but I knew for him, being a footballer, he always wanted to teach his son his football skills.

Throughout the pregnancy I used to say I think it's a girl, I just have this feeling, to throw him off. He never knew we were having a boy. It was quite fun keeping it to myself and throwing everybody off the scent when we were having conversations about the gender. Inside I was laughing to myself. We had a 3D scan and he was just wonderful. He was moving his hand across his face, pulling a face and everything, it was so beautiful. The sonographer however at one point said 'he' and Jas picked up on it. I suggested maybe that was the for the last couple she'd had in there and she'd just got confused and said it again out of habit. I told him not to pay any attention to it. Again, I was laughing inside to myself knowing how overjoyed he would be when I gave birth to a little boy.

At one of the appointments with my midwife, she noticed that my bump was looking small. She arranged for me to have a growth scan on Friday, 13 April 2012.

She laughed and said, "you're not superstitious, are you?"

I said, "a little, but I would rather know my babies OK as soon as possible."

We went to the growth scan and I was told everything was fine. The lady kept talking about a man she knew that lived at our address before us, so we remember the appointment very well.

Everything carried on as expected for the next few weeks and I had a wonderful baby shower at my parent's house which was organised by my mum, sister, one of my best friends and my younger cousin. There were lots of beautiful gender neutral gifts and we played fabulous games that had been organised by my friend. It was so much fun!

Before we knew it, it was the first day of my maternity leave Monday, 18 June 2012. I remember the day starting so nicely. I was sitting down with a cup of tea, Luca kicked me so hard and I thought to myself he's running out of room. As a big football family, I was sitting watching the football fixtures for the Premier League year ahead as they were announced on 'Sky Sports' and I was posting them on Facebook. We were getting the house ready for the baby's arrival. I had workmen in putting up blackout blinds in the bedrooms and another doing other small jobs for us. It was fair to say I was nesting.

So, the day went on and I felt his flutters here and there. He always had a quiet time in the afternoon and before we knew it; it was evening. My husband came home, and I made dinner and we carried on with the evening as we always did, dinner first and then watching some TV. The Euro's 2012 were on, so we were watching a football match. Somehow Luca always knew when the football was on and he would always kick more at that time. We used to laugh and say he or she is going to be a footballer. It was coming up to half time in the match and I remarked that the baby is a little quiet today. I thought it was strange because usually they were so active during the football. So, Jas brought me a cold drink to get the baby to be active as that had always worked previously. It didn't work this time though, so he brought me some chocolate.

"Let's wake him up," he said, " and get him to listen to the football."

This didn't work either.

So, I said, "I'll go upstairs to the bedroom," as that normally worked.

I suggested the baby was probably just running out of space to move about. It was about 9:30 p.m. at this point.

I received a message from my brother Sunny who'd gone off to work abroad for a few weeks and he texted to say he'd arrived safely. I browsed around on my phone for a little while waiting for some movement from the little one and still there was nothing. We had been into the hospital the week before too, when I thought I had a tear in my waters as I was damp in my underwear. When we went to triage and they tested me, they'd said all was fine. I was getting a little concerned by this point however, so Jas suggested we called the hospital. I was still convinced it was just the baby running out of room to move.

The day before we'd been at my parent's house as it was Father's Day, my Dad's Birthday, and my Parent's Anniversary all in one day. Luca had been really active. He was kicking, he had hiccups, and everyone had taken turns to feel my belly whilst he was moving. We laughed every time my sister put her hand on my belly, as he would stop moving, he didn't want to be active for his aunt. My sister's children were loving it and laughing, and everyone was getting excited for his arrival.

We called the hospital and they asked us to come in so they could just check to see he was okay. So, we did. There was a little wait at the hospital by the time we got there so it'd probably have been around 10:30 p.m. After waiting for around twenty minutes we were taken into a room to be monitored. The midwife connected the CTG monitor to me and brought out the scanning equipment. She began to put the gel on my tummy and started the scanning machine. She muttered about the equipment being so unpredictable at times, and that she'd get a senior midwife as she'd have better luck with the equipment.

I looked at Jas and his face was calm. The senior midwife came in and began to start scan my tummy. There was silence and I saw the staff take a glance at each other. She asked us to bear with her whilst she went to call the doctor. At this point I knew something was wrong and tears began to fill my eyes. Jas gripped my hand tightly and the doctor came in. He began to scan my belly and they all looked at each other.

The doctor said the words I will never forget that haunt me to this day, "I'm sorry."

I yelled out, "no not my baby!"

Jas fell to his knees, holding my hand, and we sobbed in disbelief that our baby had gone. The doctor told us he would leave us for a while and then come back and repeated how sorry he was. Jas and I just held each other and cried; we could not believe this was happening. Why was this happening?

When the doctor returned he sat down with us. We were still crying obviously.

I asked him, "why has this happened, why has he died?"

The doctor couldn't explain why at that point and told us that we would need to come back in the morning to have another scan, to confirm what he'd said. We were confused and wanted to know why we had to come back to have it confirmed. He explained that the procedure was to have two scans to confirm the baby's heart had stopped and as it was nearly midnight, we would need to come back in the morning. He was very empathetic and talked to us with great sympathy. He went on to explain that I would need to deliver Luca naturally, and once he was delivered he would be checked to see if there was anything wrong with him or wrong with my placenta. At this point he reiterated that he could not explain why it might have happened, but they would do everything they could to find out why for us.

We went home, not making any sense of what was happening, it felt like I was walking in a nightmare. Once we got home, we just put our arms around each other and sobbed again and then yet again. It had gone midnight by the time we got home so we went to bed soon after, but we couldn't sleep, we couldn't understand what had just happened. At that point, I felt the need to tell Jas that we were having a boy. I didn't want him to just find out at the birth, I felt he needed to know now. I explained how long I had known and why I had kept it to myself. He hugged me and told me it didn't matter, he understood that I wanted him to have a surprise.

As the night went on we dozed in and out of sleep not really resting of course just playing those words around in our heads continuously, 'I'm sorry.' The next morning arrived. Jas had gone to the bathroom and when he came back to the bedroom I was sobbing. He held me so close and wept with me again. It was probably 7:00 a.m. at this point and Jas needed to call his manager to explain what had happened. Just before that, we received a call from the hospital from the doctor we had seen the night before saying could we come in for 8:00 o'clock. Jas confirmed yes we could.

I told Jas that my mum knew I had an appointment today for a check-up and she'd be calling me later to find out how it went. You'll have to tell her now before she goes to work, I urged him. I also asked him to call my brother Steven, before he went to work as I needed him here. I'm very close to my brothers. I needed their bear hugs. Jas made the calls, first to his manager then to my mum and then Steven. It was so hard for him to make all those calls but knew he had to. Mum had already gone to work so he decided not to tell his family just yet and wait until we came back from the hospital.

We made our way to the hospital and explained to the receptionist at triage that the doctor had asked us to come in. She said that she didn't have my name on the records and Jas explained we were here last night, and the doctor called this morning to ask us to come for 8:00 o'clock so please check as he will be waiting for us. The reception wasted a lot of time and we were probably waiting around for forty to fifty minutes. By this point the doctor had left and somebody else came for us. She took us to the scanning area where I had to be scanned again to confirm that Luca's heartbeat had stopped. Inside I was praying and hoping that they'd got it wrong and actually he was fine and just hiding from us. This was not true however and it was confirmed again that his heart had stopped. The room was silent, and I sobbed again and again and again, as did Jas.

I had to see a consultant next, who explained what we needed to go through over the next few days. He gave me some tablets to take, these were to induce me and then gave me some more to take home. The midwife with him explained that we could now go home and when any contractions started or if my waters broke we should come to the hospital immediately. If that didn't happen however, I was to come back to the hospital the next morning at 10 a.m. We tried to let all the information sink in and went home. Jas had received some messages from my family, Steven, and my mum. Steven had explained to his manager what had happened and that he needed to be with his sister. They were very understanding and gave him time off to be with us. My mum was a self- employed postmistress at this time, and she had to call the headquarters, to tell them what happened and explain that she needed to close for a couple of days.

My mum had also called my sister in law Olivia, wife of my brother Sunny asking her to get a message to Sunny to explain what had happened. My mum also had to break the news to my sister who was at work and came home immediately. Around midday my mum, dad and my sister came over to my home. They all put their arms around me after having hugs with Jas and we all sobbed. My mum put her hands on my belly and questioned how this could happen as the baby had been so active on Sunday we were at theirs. She wasn't really asking the question she was just saying her thoughts out loud, trying like the rest of us to make sense of it. It was almost like she was willing him to move. After a while of them just them holding me and us all crying, we started to talk about what had happened and how it began. I explained the events of Monday night and how we had tried to get him moving and he simply hadn't and then how we had gone to the hospital. Meanwhile Jas received a message from Steven explaining that he was getting a train to my sister in law's. She lived near the station and they would then drive up together to our house.

The day went by in quite a daze. My parents and sister left and then before we knew it, Steven and Olivia were at our home. I got that Big Bear hug that I needed from Steven. I sobbed onto his sweatshirt and he kissed my head and cried with me. Olivia sat next to me, put her arm around me and we cried. She then told me that she had contacted Sunny's company and asked for him to be sent home. Whilst Steven and Olivia sat with me, Jas went to his parent's home to tell them the terrible news. When he came back his mum was with him and as my mum had done, she held me close and cried and held my belly and cried more. Jas took his mum back home about an hour later. Steven had said he was going to stay with us, which was a great relief, because I knew he would be a great support for not just me but Jas as well. Olivia said she would go back home and wait to hear from Sunny to see when he would be able to come back. Steven made us a light dinner to keep our energy up, but none of us were really in the mood to eat.

It was Wednesday, 20 June 2012, again I hadn't really slept. Thoughts had kept going around in my head, was it my fault, did I do something wrong? My body had failed my child! Feelings of guilt started setting in. I kept thinking about things I should have done and that I had done something wrong. Now I just wanted to give birth to my child and see him, I wanted to hold him in my arm. I wanted this next stage to be over as quick as possible.

My hospital bags ready, we had a light breakfast and a cup of tea and Jas's family came over. They wanted to see me before I went to the hospital, both of Jas's parents and his sister. Jas's dad hugged me so tight and just didn't want to let go, and he cried and I cried with him, It was the first time he'd ever hugged me like this, I could feel the pain and the love from him, something I'll never forget. It felt like he wanted to wrap me in cotton wool and stop me from having to go through what was next. Jas's sister also did the same and said she'd be here for me, whatever I needed.

Steven was taking us to the hospital. I'd said there was no point taking our car as there's never any parking there. We arrived at the hospital and went up to the ward. There was a private room ready for us. We were taken straight in and settled into our room. We were told a bereavement midwife would be along to see us shortly. I was given a gown to wear and then settled onto the bed with lots of cushions. Jas said he'd pay for the TV so that we could watch something whilst we waited for my waters to break and labour to start. I always like watching the 'This Morning' programme, so we watched that followed by 'Loose Women,' another one of my favourites. I was brought a jug of water and the midwives were very empathetic. They knew that I was there to give birth to my baby who had died. They ensured we were comfortable and then left us alone.

Shortly after the bereavement midwife arrived, she was a lovely lady. She sat with us and gave us lots of information, too much to take in at the time. She spoke to us about our options, one having a post -mortem, two having a footprint and some handprints of Luca. She also explained that after the birth we could go to a family suite and be able to have Luca overnight. She gave us information about bereavement support that we would be able to use in the weeks to come. There was a whole packet of information, too much to go through at the time, but something we could take home, nonetheless. Now we just had to wait for me to deliver him. After about half an hour the bereavement midwife left, and it was comforting to know that we had her to support us.

Soon it was lunchtime. There were no signs of my waters breaking or labour starting, so we were both told we could go pick some lunch. Jas and I walked down to the trolley and chose something. After lunch, Jas suggested we watch a movie together I agreed, we needed something to keep us occupied. Being big Marvel fans, we decided to watch Captain America. My mind however drifted into other things. I was thinking about delivering Luca and holding him. Then suddenly my mind started to think about what he would look like. Would he be very blue in colour, would he look like a normal baby? I didn't know what to expect. I felt like everything was out of my control, so many thoughts in my head going round and round, wondering whether the labour would be easier, just not knowing what to expect. It all just left me in a daze. My head felt foggy like I couldn't think straight, too many thoughts almost making me dizzy. In weeks to come I realised my thoughts were quite normal, but by now I knew that once Luca was delivered, I wanted his nappy and clothes put on him, the ones that were in my hospital bag.

It was now around 5:30 to 6 o'clock in the evening, we'd had some dinner and then my waters broke. Jas called for the midwife and she told us it was time to go down to the labour ward. Here goes I thought! Almost immediately my contractions started, and they were getting stronger by the time I reached the labour ward. Within it seemed like only ten minutes, I was screaming with pain. Gas and air was doing nothing for me.

The midwife asked, "do you want an epidural?"

I replied," yes," and they went to call for an anaesthetist.

When he arrived, he tried to administer the epidural, however it didn't work the first time and my gosh, it was painful. I never thought I'd be one of those women that was screaming in labour, but I was. He tried to administer it again, and again it didn't work. After six attempts and me screaming with pain, Jas was getting angry and worried. The midwife recommended they call a senior anaesthetist; I had no idea we had a junior one. My gosh, was I not going through enough giving birth to my sleeping child? Now they give me a junior who couldn't even administer this! What on earth were they thinking? The senior one promptly arrived and administered the epidural all in one quick go…the seventh attempt had worked.

After having about four or five people in the room with us whilst the epidural was being administered we were now just down to the midwife. This midwife that stayed with us throughout my labour. She was fantastic. She explained to me that because I'd had the epidural I would not feel the contractions, so she would check regularly to see how dilated I was and how strong the contractions were. I lay back on my bed waiting for nature to take its course. The farce with the epidural had made me feel quite poorly and unfortunately my earlier dinner came up.

By around 8:30 p.m. I was willing Luca to come out. The next day would be the birthdays of my sister in law Olivia and Jas's eldest nephew. I was thinking they don't really need to be sharing their birthday with Luca who's never going to be here to celebrate his birthday alongside them. It's strange how your mind thinks when you are always caring about others even at the point of when you're giving birth to your stillborn baby. Nothing was really happening in terms of contractions and dilation, it felt like I was just waiting forever. Being on the main labour ward I could hear the cries of other babies being born and mothers giving birth. It broke my heart knowing that my baby was going to come out with no cry at all. It was so hard to hear, not that I begrudged other people having their babies, quite the contrary, it was just hard for me at that time giving birth, but not going to have my baby and hear him making those beautiful crying sounds.

The midwife came in and out throughout the evening and night to see if I was dilating more. I had and she thought she'd seen Luca's hand so went to get a doctor to check if this was going to make delivery hard. It was the same doctor that had pronounced Luca dead on Monday night. It was good to know that we were in safe hands as he was a really nice doctor. He checked and everything was OK, so it would be a normal delivery. He continued to speak with us and sat with us for a while. He asked why we didn't arrive early on Tuesday and we explained we had but that the receptionist had been extremely hard to get by and was adamant that we had no appointment. He then wanted to know which receptionist, what she looked like etc. I didn't know her name but described her anyway and he rolled his eyes as if they've had lots of problems with this receptionist in the past. He explained that he knew who she was and that he'd be having words.

He reiterated that when I'd delivered our son they would be looking for signs of anything that may of caused his death. This could be the cord wrapped around his neck which was the most common reason. They would also look at my placenta see if there were any blockages or clots that could be signs of why Luca had passed. He said then the next option you have, if all is OK, is to have a post-mortem, if you wish to find out more details of his passing. We already knew we wanted to do this, we needed to know why our baby had died. We had gone through this with the bereavement midwife already and had made the decision together.

He then started talking about the future and the different levels of grieving that we would go through. The anger we'd display, the acceptance, the continuing grief. He said that if we decided to have children in the future I'd be monitored a lot more closely and they would ensure I had an obstetrician that I felt comfortable with. He said there were a number of great obstetricians at the hospital and he mentioned a few of them. He said there was one lady who scans all the time, at every appointment and there was another who would take care of me in other ways. I knew when he said about the one that scans all the time that would be the one I would want for sure. Obviously at this point I wasn't really thinking about having another child, I was just concerned about delivering my child now and holding him in my arms for as long as I could. After sitting with us for about forty minutes the doctor was called to another patient and he wished us all the best under the circumstances. It had just gone midnight; Jas and I were drifting in and out of sleep constantly. It was hard to sleep as it was a noisy labour ward of course.

Before we knew it was around 7:15 a.m. on 21 June 2012. I had fully dilated, and my contractions were stronger, the midwife said that it was time to deliver our baby. She was the same midwife that had been with us throughout the night. She was lovely. Another midwife came in and explained she was going to assist with the delivery around 7.40 a.m. I couldn't feel my contractions because of the epidural so they explained that they would monitor when my contractions were happening and then tell me to push. It felt like I was pushing for ages, in reality it was probably twenty minutes, certainly not that long. Jas held my hand and supported me whilst I was pushing. The midwife encouraged me to do one last big push, give it everything I'd got. Then, she said, he was here.

There was an awful silence, and I cried, we both did. The midwife that had been with us all night should have been off duty by now, but God bless her she stayed as she wanted to be there when I delivered Luca.

"He's beautiful," said the midwife, and she showed him to me.

My gosh yes he was just beautiful. I didn't hold him straight away. I still had that thing in my head, I needed him in his clothes and his nappy. It wasn't like I was having skin to skin contact with him was it, which I would have done ordinarily. The second midwife now took over and explained that she'd get him cleaned up for us and then bring him back. In the meantime, they were taking my placenta out well at least trying to take my placenta out. They called the doctor as my placenta seemed to be stuck. I thought this was why my baby had passed that there's something wrong with my placenta. The doctor (a different one by this time) couldn't detach the placenta and told me I would need to go to theatre for it to be done.

I asked, "is this normal, is this why my son has passed?"

She replied," this does happen sometimes but it's not a reason why a baby would pass."

She explained however, that when they took my placenta out they would be checking it for clots and any blockages.

Whilst they were getting things ready for me to go to theatre, I suggested that Jas had some time with Luca whilst I was there. He said he would do, and he'd also call our parents just to let them know that he had been delivered and let them know later when they can come to see him. I was wheeled off to theatre to get the placenta detached and taken out and Jas was left in the room alone. The midwife had been called to another mother in labour, but she assured, me that Luca would be with us soon. So, there was I in theatre, having the placenta taken out and once it was out they checked it and found no blockages or no clots. I asked what would happen next and they told me they would send the placenta to be examined more thoroughly. Clearly it wasn't my placenta that had failed Luca, so what could it be?

I was taken back to the labour ward and Jas was waiting in the room.

I asked, "where's Luca?"

His eyes were red. I wasn't sure whether he'd been crying or whether it was from the lack of sleep.

I asked again, "what's the matter where's Luca?"

Jas replied, "I'm not sure."

I said," haven't you asked anybody?"

He said," yes. I went out to call our parents and then came back hoping Luca would be here, but as he wasn't I went out to the desk and asked if I could have him."

He breathed deeply and explained the midwife outside, an Asian lady had asked him if he was the father of the dead baby?

In utter shock, I gasped and said, "she said what!!"

Clearly Jas had been crying because of this most insensitive woman who clearly was in the wrong job if she could speak such unkind words. I choked up thinking what he must have felt when she said that to him, clearly the same as I was now feeling having heard it. How can someone in this profession be so vile with their words, I could not comprehend this.

By now we were watching the clock, I was wondering where on earth Luca was. Every time a midwife came by we would ask them if we could have our son? Each time we got the reply, yes, they'd see what I can do. It was now lunchtime, so we had a couple of sandwiches, and I had a cup of tea. Right now, that we've eaten, we want our son I thought. I had given birth to him just after 8 o'clock and it was now after lunchtime and he still wasn't with us, where was he? I was becoming more and more frustrated. We had been left alone now for a couple of hours. Jas had gone out to the desk again, but no one was there for him to ask. So, we just waited and waited and waited, it was ridiculous. This was precious time we should have been having with our son and wasn't even with us.

Around 4 p.m. our bereavement midwife came in to see us. The first thing I said to her was that we hadn't seen Luca since this morning, when I delivered him. She was shocked and said she'd go and find out what was happening and where he was. She came back a few minutes later apparently he was in the room next door and now the paediatricians were with him checking him over. She said she'd go and get his handprints and footprints whilst they checked him. All this time, eight hours it had been now, and he had been next door to us laying there in the next room whilst we were elsewhere waiting for him, and nobody was able to bring him to us. What on earth had they been doing? Surely if they knew he was next door they could have just wheeled him into the room for us? It would have taken them less than a minute to do it and eight hours later we find out this. We were fuming, we couldn't believe he had been treated in such a way. Within half an hour the bereavement midwife wheeled in Luca in his cot. Finally, our son was with us!

She took him out the cot and placed him in my arms. I smiled at him, he was beautiful and then I wept. Jas touched his head and kissed him. He was perfect, there was nothing wrong with him that we could see. I asked the bereavement midwife what the what the paediatricians had said. She said that they had measured him, had checked him over and there was nothing that they could find wrong with him. She said he really was a beautiful boy and I nodded in agreement. She said now let me go and find out if we can get you up to a family room and then you can call your family to come and meet Luca once you've settled. At this point I thought there's no way you're taking him out of my arms now it's taken eight hours for us to get him nearly nine really. Jas obviously wanted to hold Luca now as well, so I passed him over gently. There was a blood stain on his nose and the bereavement midwife explained it would have been caused when the paediatricians were checking him. This made me feel like he was very fragile, so I was extra gentle when passing him to Jas. Jas wept holding Luca in his arms our first child our son, he was a much wanted and loved baby from the moment of conception. The midwife came back and said that the family room was ready for us and they said they'd take me up in a wheelchair and I asked to hold Luca whist we went up. She said she would place Luca in a Moses basket and bring him up to the room once we were there. I made it clear that as our time with Luca had been made shorter by the incompetence of the staff not bringing him to us, I didn't want to wait any longer and for there to be any more delays now! She assured me it would be as soon as possible when we were in our room.

My wheelchair was brought round, and I was helped into it. I held a memory box that we had been given to keep Luca's things in. Jas carried the bags and we were taken up to a ward. We had to go past the main reception in triage just outside the labour ward. There were lots of parents and expectant mums sitting there looking at us as we went by. Clearly they could see that we'd been crying but they had no idea what we had been going through. When we got up to the ward, we were taken into the family room. It had a double bed, a TV, an ensuite. It was almost like a hotel room really. Jas had called our families to inform them that they could come to the hospital now, and which ward they should come up to. Luca was a little blue in the lips and around his face and for some reason I felt like I needed to tell my family this, so they didn't feel shocked when they saw him. Again, thinking about other people's feelings how stupid am I? I texted Steven and asked him to tell everybody that Luca was a little bit blue so they wouldn't be too shocked. I didn't know what they'd really be expecting. He said they'd be there soon. As we settled down, I looked at the room and thought to myself, why could I not have given birth to Luca in this room. It was private and away from the labour ward, that way I would not have had to hear all the other babies being born and crying!

Jas's family arrived first. Luca wasn't in the room by this point, so they sat on some seats waiting and asking how it had been. I think I was all cried out by now, and I asked how their children were. The door opened then, and Luca was brought in by the midwife in a Moses basket. Another midwife was holding the stand and they placed it next to my bed and then put Luca in. My mother in law was the first one to get up to look at him and she smiled and said he looked like my brother Steven. Obviously if he looked like Steven that meant he looked like me I thought. Tears filled her eyes, her first grandson from her eldest son, but there was no joy, just heartbreak at the thought that he had died. Jas's sister wanted to take a couple of photos to show her sons and I said that was fine, so she did, and she also said how gorgeous he was. Within a few minutes my family had arrived, my parents my grandma, Steven and my sister. My grandma, my nanny, was Luca's only remaining great grandparent. The first thing she did was held me in her arms and I wept on her shoulder. My parents cried as they looked at Luca. My mum said he was perfect and gorgeous. The families paid their condolences to each other whilst in the room and then everyone just looked at Luca. Conversations went on, but I'm not really sure what they were about, I can't remember. One thing I do remember though is that as they were talking no one took their eyes off Luca. My mom sat next to me on the bed and held my hand, showing me the love, you can only get from your mother. I could feel it just by holding hands.

At around 7:30 p.m. Jas's family left but my family said they would stay until 8 p.m. which was the end of normal visiting hours. My dad took some photos of Luca and then he asked if he could hold him. I really wanted to say yes, but knowing that his nose had bled earlier, I said I think he's a bit fragile and explained what had happened earlier. He said OK, don't worry. My mum spoke to Luca saying how delighted and excited they were when they knew that I was having him, and she cried. I knew she was crying whilst holding my hand and talking to Luca. It was grief for Luca but also because of what her daughter was going through too. 8:00 p.m. came and my family had to leave. Each one of them gave Luca a kiss on his head knowing that they'd not see him again. I asked my sister to call two of my best friends to inform them of what had happened and she said she would. My family hugged Jas and I, and mum said to try and get some sleep. Clearly I had massive bags under my eyes from the lack of sleep and obviously from crying with grief for my son. Before leaving mum said Sunny was also here, that he was able to come back and he'd come to see us tomorrow if that was OK. I said that'd be lovely.

Now it was just the three of us: Jas, Luca and I. I took him out of his Moses basket and held him close, then Jas held him, and we took it in turns a couple of times. A midwife came in to give me some painkillers as I had a painful headache understandably. She asked Jas if he was OK, if he needed any paracetamol and he said no he was OK. She brought us a jug of water and then left us for the night. She said if we needed anything we should just press the buzzer and she closed the door. I placed Luca back in his cot and I went to bathroom to put my pyjamas on, brush my teeth and pass water for the first time that day, as I'd had had a catheter in all this time. I went back into my room and lay down, Jas lay next to me, holding me close whilst we both just looked at Luca. Time to get some sleep I said, we are both exhausted. Jas agreed and we dimmed the lights and fell asleep.

On Friday, 22 June 2012, we woke up at around 7:30 a.m. I had been waking during the night, checking on Luca. How strange, but a mother's instinct had already crept in, and I was doing those natural things that we do as mothers, checking our babies. But what was I really checking on, he wasn't alive, but my motherly feelings still made me wake, check on him, look at him, at his still body. The breakfast trolley was outside. The midwife came in and asked if we'd like some breakfast. We said we would and Jas said he'd come and get it. Jas asked me what I would like, and I replied that I'd have a small amount of cereal and a cup of tea please.

So, we had our breakfast and then the midwife came back in and said they would give us a couple more hours with our baby and someone would come to speak to us about signing the post-mortem forms. A couple of hours is that all, is that really all we have with Luca, a couple more hours? I couldn't believe it. It had taken us nearly nine hours to get him back with us yesterday, we've had him overnight yes, but we were sleeping and now just a couple more hours. I took Luca out of the Moses basket knowing these couple of hours were going to be so precious and nowhere near enough. I walked around with him. Again, that motherly instinct, that feeling, was making me do things that didn't really make sense. I was rocking him in my arms I didn't even realise it for a few minutes, but it just felt natural holding my baby in my arms and rocking him. Well that is what mothers do, and clearly my inner motherhood wanted to do the same, so I carried on doing it and it felt nice in a strange way. The midwife came back and I asked why we could only have a couple of hours with him and she replied that it was because his body would deteriorate if he wasn't put in a cold container. Woah, a cold container, words I did not like hearing, but unfortunately this was our reality. I knew she was right, there was a slight odour coming from Luca's mouth. It wasn't horrible, but I understood that it would become worse over time even over hours. It just didn't feel fair, it had taken us so long to get him back with us yesterday through no fault of our own but because of staff on the labour ward who clearly ignored us. Now we needed to make the most of these two hours. Jas and I took it in turns to hold Luca and I took a few photos of him in his Moses basket looking sound asleep. His skin was clearing a bit today, he wasn't looking quite so blue. He was gorgeous. My grandma had said the night before he was too gorgeous for this world, maybe she was right, but it didn't soften the blow though. In my head all I could think about was holding him for as long as I could, we knew we hadn't got very long. I asked Jas if I should take a photo of him in your arms and he said if I did when he looked back at the photos it would make him cry and I thought yes quite true, therefore we didn't.

At times like this when you're told you only got a couple of hours with your child, a child that you're never going to see again, the child that you love with all your heart, you can't really think clearly. Like I said all we thought about was just holding him. Whilst I held him a doctor came in and wanted to go through the paperwork for the post-mortem. We listened and said yes and then whilst Jas held Luca the doctor said he'd leave the paperwork here and come back later we could have a chance to read through it.

It was almost 10 o'clock and the midwife came in and said, "shall we take him?"

I nodded but in my inside I as saying no, not yet. I took Luca from Jas's arms and held him tight against me to my chest so that I could smell his hair and kiss his head. I could feel the anxiety building inside me because I didn't want to let him go. In my head I kept thinking they're going to take my baby soon, he's my baby this isn't how things should be. Mother Nature has gone wrong horribly wrong. I should be looking forward to taking my son home now not dreading them taking him to the mortuary.

Twenty minutes passed, the midwife came again and asked, "are you ready now?"

I shook my head and said, "no!"

Jas could see that I was not going to let her take him and that I would keep delaying them.

He said," Shaz, we are going to have to let them take him, I know we don't want to, but we will have to."

I nodded my head in agreement not that I really agreed at all. This just isn't long enough with our baby I thought I can't just let him go now. Clearly I had no choice though and it felt like my heart was being ripped out of my body with all this pain that I was feeling now, having to give him away. It was already building, my breathing was getting heavier I didn't want to do this. "I'm not going to see him again," I said to Jas. "I know baby" he said, "and this is going to be very hard."

We had him for another twenty minutes or so, I held him, kissing him, kissing his hands, his head, his cheeks, even his cute little button nose and then finally a little kiss on his lips. I told Luca that I was I'm always going to be his mummy and promised him he would always live on as long as I was alive, that his name and his memory would stay alive. Jas had his arm around me and a hand on Luca, he kissed his cheeks, and said I love you my baby boy. We both cried knowing that these were the last few moments we had with him. I can't do this I said to Jas, how am I going to give him up. We won't see him again, I said to him. I was finding it hard to get my words out, I was just crying so much. Jas said through his tears, I know babe we're never going to see him again, let's remember his face, his little hands and hug him tight now. Jas held and hugged Luca and I so close to him, and then the door opened. There was the midwife again, she looked at us and asked if she could take him, I didn't reply but Jas nodded to her. She came close, I was still holding Luca and I stood up to put him in his Moses basket but before I did I had one last tight hug, kissed his head and his cheeks and said to him, I love you with all my heart my baby boy and always will, as I placed him back into his Moses basket. I broke down in tears as she carried him away, my baby,

37

no, my baby!! Jas threw his arms around me and we sat on the bed sobbing and sobbing uncontrollably together.

After ten minutes or so the doctor came back for the post-mortem forms. We hadn't really read them I said, he replied that's OK I've explained everything that's in there anyway. Jas had a glance over the forms and agreed. We both signed them and asked how long it would take. The doctor explained it varied but as he was a baby it shouldn't be too long. He said they would keep in contact with our funeral directors and let them know when our son would arrive after the post-mortem.

Jas called Steven and asked him to come and pick us up. Let's just go home now he said, OK I replied as I put my things in the bag. The midwife came in and we explained that we'd be going home now. She said OK and that she had some medicines for me to take, then she handed me some tablets and explained that the midwife would be in contact with me as they would still need to check me as with any new mother at home. Wow I wasn't really expecting that, to have visits from my midwife. She said it was standard procedure and that they always have to check after a mother has given birth.

Steven arrived and we were ready to leave, so we made our way downstairs. He had parked as close as he could and as soon as we got in the car, he drove off. As we were leaving, I looked back at the hospital through the rear window, and my eyes filled with tears. I'm leaving the hospital without my baby and he's been taken to the mortuary. I cried and Jas put his hand around mine. When we arrived home, I cried thinking about the fact that I was walking into my house without my baby boy, and I felt so empty, this was not the way things should have been.

Shortly after arriving home Steven made me a cup of tea and we just sat and watched television. There was a knock at the door. It was a delivery, gosh what timing. The delivery was the travel system we had ordered for Luca, his pushchair, and his car seat with the ISOFIX. Jas asked the delivery guy to place the things in our converted garage. The gentleman said, you are going to have your hands full soon and Jas just slightly smiled and thanked him for the delivery. Inside his heart was breaking seeing everything we had ordered for Luca being delivered, but he did not have the heart to say actually no our baby had died. I cried again, I had forgotten that delivery was coming today, everything just felt so unfair, why had this happened? I felt like I was living in a nightmare, that just was not ending. Jas came back in and put his arm around me and shed some tears himself too.

My mum had messaged Steven to say that they were going to bring some food over and pop in and see me. My brother Sunny and his wife were also coming and my sister and her family too. When Sunny arrived, he gave me a Big Bear hug and I wept in his arms and he kissed my forehead and said I'm so sorry sis. We had a little time just us five, before mum, my sister and her family arrived. Our small house was suddenly full of people but not the person that I wanted the most, Luca. I felt like I was in a daze. Conversations were happening around me, but I wasn't present. It felt like I was on another planet. A planet of grief, confusion, emptiness, hurt. I was heartbroken, something completely unknown by me. Suddenly I was back in the room and my nephew was laughing at something my brother Sunny had said. My nephew had a cute loud laugh and it was pleasant to hear, although at this time in particular it felt strange. I suddenly realised that I was actually feeling quite a headache coming on and felt exhausted and said I needed to lay down. I said to my mum, "please just leave us enough food to eat later and come back tomorrow." I felt a little bad that I was saying this as I know their actions and thoughts were only in my interest, but it was a little too soon to have everyone together. Mum understood and said, "it's OK my sweetheart I wasn't sure whether it would help to have us all or not. We'll come again tomorrow, and I'll make you something different to eat, but I've left enough food for you all to have tonight." She knew my favourite was her lasagne. They all gave me huge hugs and went on their way and Sunny said he'd be in contact whilst he was away and to take care sis and he loved me.

The following day Jas's parents came to visit, and his mum bought us some food. They sat for a while, as they did several times over the next few weeks too. Over the next few days, we kept receiving messages of condolences from people, some I didn't even have a number or name for, so I just kindly replied with thank you for your kind words. Five days after Luca's birth someone in Jas's family had a baby boy. It was a relief to know the baby had arrived safely, there were no tears just gladness in our hearts for the parents.

We had a few close friends and cousins coming and going over the next few weeks and we waited to hear the news that Luca's body had been being released from the post -mortem and we could set his funeral date. Over these weeks, whilst waiting to organise the funeral, thoughts constantly kept going around in my head, wondering what had I done wrong, how did I fail my baby? I wasn't sleeping very well and had come out with a rash all over my body and on my face. It looked like an allergic reaction to the medication or something I had eaten, so I had to go to the doctors and Jas drove me there.

When I saw the doctor, I sat down and she said, "Oh you don't look over thirty-six weeks pregnant."

We just looked at each other. Jas told her our baby was stillborn. I began to cry, and she said she was so sorry she hadn't been informed. She spoke for a while about bereavement and I explained the reason I'd gone in. I think she could tell from my eyes I hadn't been sleeping, so she gave me some light sleeping pills which I had for a week to ten days. It made me realise that you assume that your GP would be told about your tragic loss, yet they had no idea. I wondered whether this was a failure in the system or just the way things are. Maybe I was just focussing on these things to try and make things easier for myself, trying to get my head around it all. I couldn't face going to the chemist for my prescription, so Jas went for me. I said to him that they knew me very well so he would have to tell them that Luca had passed away. When he came back he said they were utterly shocked and cried and said they sent their regards to me.

The tablets helped me sleep over the coming days and helped get my body used to a new timetable. Our closest friends came to visit us. One said, "I don't know what to say!" Jas replied, "the fact you are here says it all for us." Two weeks after my son had died, someone brought a wedding invitation to our house. My thoughts were do you seriously think I'm going to dress up for a wedding when my son has just died. I felt like screaming ARE YOU SERIOUS! But no, I kept quiet, but I was raging inside. Apparently the groom's parents had insisted we had the invitation, in case by then I was up to going. ERM NO!! I wanted to shout.

It was quite repetitive over the coming weeks, having well-wishers come by and receiving messages. My best friends, our joint best friends, and closest family members were the ones we allowed to come. It was comforting to see how much support and love we had from our visitors, many didn't know what to say but the fact that they were just there, meant a lot to us. Steven had started fundraising in Luca's memory to fund a baby charity. Our neighbours, friends, and family all donated money and he raised over £1,500. I barely left the house for weeks as I just couldn't face people and the outside world. I was feeling increasingly more empty and lonely. My arms felt like I should be holding my baby, but instead they were empty. In my mind I would constantly be thinking what I would be doing if Luca had been alive. I was growing increasingly depressed and cried every day.

Summary

If you are taken to the Labour ward to give birth to your sleeping baby, then ask (insist) on being taken to the bereavement family room to give birth away from all the heartbreak of hearing other babies being born alive.

It's very important at this stage in the family room or any room you are in, to ask for a cuddle cot if it has not already been offered! This equipment will gift you the extra time you need to say your goodbyes to your little angel baby.

From this first chapter, I would like you to understand the key points I am trying to make as I tell my story. The mother of a stillborn will still have motherly instincts and will still have her post-pregnancy body. This will make her feel increasingly depressed, empty, and lonely. When I say lonely, I mean loneliness because she is without her baby, not loneliness because people aren't around her. If you are a mother in baby loss reading this, then know that you are not alone in these feelings that you will be having. Those feelings will be of anger, grief, loneliness, emptiness, walking in a nightmare, heartache, tears, suicidal thoughts, depression, anxiety, wanting to be alone, wanting people with you, fear, anguish, and much more, but know that these feelings are perfectly fine.

If you are somebody supporting a person in baby loss, whether it be the mother or father or another member of the family, please put yourself in their shoes. It's hard to imagine losing your child, but if you are a parent, just try and imagine the horror and trauma of your child passing away. Imagine the things that would cause you pain when said by other people; now learn from that and please don't say them to the Angel Warrior are that you are supporting. Understand that at times they will be wanting to talk, not wanting to talk, they might appear like they're back to the normal, but know that they will never be back to the old normal that they were. You will be supporting their new normal. Give them a shoulder to cry on, let them feel they can talk openly and just listen, you don't have to always respond. Sit in silence with them just watching TV maybe.

Do not say it was meant to be, it is part of God's plan, you can have another child, at least you are healthy, at least you have other children, when will you have another baby, you need to move on, look to the future, you need to get out, have faith, at least it happened now.

Support them with, would you like to go out, shall I make you some food, shall we have a cup of tea and just sit and watch television, what would you like to do, is there anything I can help with, shall I do the ironing for you, is there anything that needs doing at home, simply be helpful.

Chapter Two
The Last Goodbye

We were now getting ready for the funeral. We had gone to florist to order some flowers, one that said son and one that said Luca. With the one that said Luca there was an attachment to it which said aunts, uncles, grandparents, cousins, because it was collectively from the family. We didn't really want too many flowers for his tiny coffin, so we decided just to do it like that. There was no point in having separate ones for grandson, nephew etc so we just stuck to the two.

We noticed that every time we went out it was to do something for the funeral. At this point, this was the only time I went out of the house really. The pouring out of empathy from the people we were talking to was very apparent. You could see on their faces that they were thinking, 'this poor couple, what must they be going through.' It was true, we were going through hell. It's the kind of journey that you never ever expect to go on. The type you never know how you can actually deal with, but somehow we had to. Believe me, it wasn't easy, and it still isn't actually, but you learn to live day by day and just take it day by day. I couldn't tell anybody what was going through my head, as no one was really going to understand. At times all I wanted to do was scream, shout and cry with sorrow and anger.

At times I did want to say to people, ''well you have a child right, imagine if your child died how would you feel?'' I was never going to say those words however, I've never been one to be so blunt. I felt like if I said those words, people would respond by saying, ''how dare you bring my child into it.'' Really I just wanted people to understand. If they could put themselves in my shoes and think about their child dying, they might just get a glimpse into how I was feeling. I wasn't wishing it upon them, these were just my thoughts about trying to help people to understand, but I never said it.

That is a problem in our society, we cannot actually say what we want to, even at our darkest time. This is why we have so much depression and mental health issues in our world. Sometimes, I just wanted to wear a top that said, 'my son just died', so people would understand why I was not a happy and bubbly person and looked at them blankly. Wearing a top would have been easier than saying it. There are no such things like that, but maybe there should be.

This is the point, I felt that a bereaved parent needed an understandable title. We are warriors, going through the hell of grief whilst our angels are in the sky. That's where my phrase 'Angel Warrior', came from way back in 2012. I was broken, not feeling like a person anymore, but more like a zombie just going through the stages of life. To me everything looked grey, there was no colour in the world for me anymore. I couldn't hear the birds; the sun would shine but not in the wonderful way I would have enjoyed it before. Life had lost all meaning.

Some days Jas needed to get out and I understood that, so he'd go and play golf with one of his best friends. I knew he needed that release as much as I hated being left alone at home. I knew it would be good for him. Whilst he was out I would always, think about what we'd be doing if Luca were here. He'd be sleeping of course; he would have been a newborn. I was always thinking about the things I should have been doing if he were here, instead of the things I was doing. At this time people were still finding out about what had happened. I was still receiving sympathy cards through the post, some from distant family members, some from distant friends and some from people that I had not really imagined getting a card from. It was nice to know that they were thinking of us.

As the funeral approached Steven returned from London and came to stay with us for a couple of days before. I don't really know what I was feeling at this time, apart from the fact it wasn't how I wanted to be feeling. I wanted Luca's casket to come into the house and for Jas and I to have some time alone with him. The night before the funeral I wasn't very hungry, I was really feeling anxious by now. I had every right to be grieving and crying and everything about my son's funeral but I suppose I was worried I would collapse completely. I thought about whether I going to manage, how I was going to say my final goodbye to my son. I knew I couldn't see him and that his body had deteriorated so much by now, the funeral directors have already told us that. I felt even more empty and kept thinking I couldn't do it, I just couldn't do it, it was too big, and I wasn't ready. It's not like you can put it off forever though, me not being ready wasn't going to help, because the day was set and everything was in place, so I couldn't suddenly say no. I felt sick and just wanted to curl up in a corner and die rather than have to go to my own sons funeral. I still had all those doubts in my head about what I had done wrong and how have I failed my son. I felt it should be me in the coffin not him. This wasn't fair, what had we ever done to deserve this kind of pain. A pain that is so deep it cuts through you and you feel it in every fibre of your body and like your heart been ripped apart. Our world had been thrown upside down. I no longer felt like a living person.

The morning of the funeral arrived. I had decided to wear one of my maternity tunics which I had been so comfortable in, feeling Luca move whilst he was alive in my stomach. It was made of pastel colours and as it was quite warm, I wore it with black leggings and a long black cardigan. Everyone began to arrive. There was just our parents, our siblings, and their partners. We didn't chat much, everyone was feeling quite anxious I think. None of us had been to a funeral for a baby. I said hello to everyone and then sat in a corner waiting for the funeral car to arrive. I stood up when it did and Jas looked at me for confirmation, we had already agreed that he would carry Luca's coffin into the house. In a way it was the last time he was ever going to carry his son. As I saw him approaching the front door carrying Lucas casket I burst into uncontrollable tears. Our son shouldn't be coming home for the first time in a box. He should have been in our arms when we arrived home after his birth.

The funeral driver laid out a stand on which Luca's coffin could sit. Jas came over to me after laying down Luca's casket and we both sobbed in each other's arms whilst everyone else sobbed too. After a short while Jas's dad asked if they should leave us alone with him, we nodded, and everyone made their way outside and stood on our driveway. Jas and I sat next to Luca's coffin. We each put one hand on his coffin and held hands with the other. We spoke to him about how active he always was in this room especially when the football was on. We told him would be the last time he'd be in here, but it was his favourite room by far. We told him about all the plans that we'd had for him when he came home, the way he should have been in our arms alive. I told him about deliveries that had already arrived for him that he could not use. I promised I would always keep his name and memory alive and that this was never going to be goodbye forever because one day we would meet again, when my life here on earth is over. I told him that I didn't want to say goodbye, it was too hard for me to do and that I just wanted to tell him that I would love him forever, miss him forever and that a piece of my heart was going with him.

Just as I finished saying that Jas's dad came into the room and asked if we were ready to go. We told him we were and that we had said everything that we could. The funeral driver carried out Luca's coffin and someone else packed up the stand and took it out. It was a sunny day, but I didn't want to take my sunglasses. As I walked out of my house, my dad put his arm around me and walked me to the funeral car. Jas needed to lock up the house. When it's a baby's funeral you don't get a hearse, it is just a funeral car. I got into the back and was followed by Jas and then my mum. Luca's casket was passed to us so that we could hold him all the way to the crematorium. His flowers were put behind us and could be seen out of the windows. His other three grandparents sat in front of us. Everyone else made their way in their own cars. I could see the shadows of my neighbours looking at a us from a distance, within their houses as we drove off.

We had picked out a couple of songs that felt right for us, so as we've reached the crematorium, the doors opened, and the Ed Sheeran song 'Little Bump' was playing. We followed behind Luca's coffin as he was placed on what looked like a large table as we all took our seats. The funeral was done by the hospital chaplain and was so beautifully spoken, the words could not have been more true. As the chaplain finished, he encouraged us to say our final goodbyes whilst music played in the background. Jas and I held hands and walked towards Luca. I put my arms around his coffin and put my head on top sobbing.

I said to him, "this is it now son, you've got to go, much as I so don't want you to. I love you so much and if crying could bring you back, you would already be back by now."

I kissed his coffin a few times, Jas did the same. We both sobbed our hearts out and could see some of the family doing the same. I couldn't take my arms off his coffin because I knew that would be the last time I'd be holding him albeit he was in his casket. Eventually Jas had to tell me to let go. I refused, saying I didn't want to, so he held me for short while as I put my head on his coffin again.

I said, "bye for now my beautiful boy, I will see you again one day when you are older as a grown-up Angel in heaven. I will always be your mummy and you will always be my first baby," as I kissed his coffin again for the last time.

Jas and I walked to our seats. I nodded to let his grandparents know they could now say their goodbyes too. Couple by couple they went up and said their goodbyes.

The chaplain gave me a look as if to ask if it was okay, and I nodded. Then, the curtain closed around Luca's coffin and then he was out of sight. My heart broke yet again. There are no words for the magnitude of pain you feel at your child's funeral. My legs felt like jelly and I held onto Jas.

We walked out slowly. His flowers were against the wall and everyone was taking their time to read the little notes that were on there. We shook hands with the chaplain and thanked him for a lovely service. The funeral car driver was ready to take us on to our next destination. As Jas is Sikh his mum had arranged for some prayers at a small temple, along with a few of his uncles and aunts. On arrival naturally, all the relatives came towards us to give us hugs of condolence. We thanked the funeral car driver and his colleague as they were to leave us there now. We sat inside and listened to what was said. Unfortunately, the priest had not taken on board that Luca had not taken a breath in this world. His speech and prayer included that he had, which I found quite disappointing.

After some food we made our way back home with my family. Jas's family stayed on at the temple. I wanted to go to the cathedral and light some candles for Luca. Everyone said it was a good idea, so we all went together. I spent a little time alone to one side of the cathedral just saying my own prayers about the day. I thanked God for giving me the strength I'd needed for the day and prayed that he would walk with me as I carried on through these dark days.

An hour or so later we were back home, and my family said they would leave us to it. They gave us hugs and mum as usual had given us food so that she could ensure we would eat that evening. Then, suddenly it was just the two of us. We spoke about how lovely the chaplain's service was and that we were blessed with nice weather. We weren't actually hungry, so we just had a light meal and watched a little TV. Then I made my way to bed as I was exhausted. Jas followed me up about half an hour later.

Jas had another two weeks off work. In total he had six weeks off with me, which was very good of his company. In those two weeks however, it became quite obvious that people were expecting us to move on now that we'd had Lucas funeral. So, there was a party going to happen the following month for the baby that was born shortly after Luca died. Needless to say, we were not in any sort of party mood. We were getting some pressure from Jas's mum however to attend the party, because they were close family she thought we should be there. She is and always has been, the one to want to always please others and cares very much about what others would say. We however, are quite the opposite. At the same time the mother of the child came to see me and said that we didn't need to attend the party as she knew we wouldn't want to and that it also wouldn't have been fair on the other guest as they would feel they couldn't celebrate the birth of her child if we were there as they would be feeling sorry for us. I was a little taken aback by the words she said although, I already knew her to be quite heartless at the best of times. It had taken her a week to text me condolences when Luca had died. I sort of understood as well, but it was clear she was saying it more so that we wouldn't be there to spoil her party. I was fine with it. I said we wouldn't be coming, and that no offence was meant, it just wasn't the right time for us to go out as we'd just cremated our son. People can really show their real colours through the words that they use when you are grieving and still at your darkest time. She was just making sure we wouldn't go and spoil their party. I hadn't wanted to go anyway, but the words she used, and her body language were hurtful.

Over these couple of weeks, Jas and I did what we could to support each and cried a lot. I did suggest to Jas that perhaps we needed to go and see the little baby as they were close family and it might be best done before their party. He agreed we'd go one Sunday. When we did go, we didn't purchase lots of gifts but gave them a hundred pounds for them to buy a couple of things for their son, so he wouldn't feel left out. We made it a quick visit. They handed me the baby and I felt obliged to hold him, but I just burst into tears. I should have been holding my own baby. He should've been here, and we should have all been happy together. By no means did I mean this in any sort of begrudging way, I was delighted for them that they had their healthy son but that didn't change the fact that mine wasn't here, and I felt it immensely. We left soon after and when I came home I just went and lay on my bed. I sobbed for so long uncontrollably. Jas asked what he could do to help, and I shouted that the only thing that would help would be to bring my baby back.

"Can you bring him back, that's what I need, I don't need anything else, I just need my baby, can you do that for me? I yelled.

Of course, he couldn't, so I shouted some more, "then there's nothing you can do for me, just leave me alone," and I carried on sobbing.

It wasn't him that I was angry at. It wasn't his fault obviously. He was mourning too. It was just asking about what he could do, at that moment, that was just too much. I snapped because all I really wanted was my baby. If anybody asked the same thing, about how they could help, in my head I would always be thinking that all I wanted was my baby and that's all you can do for me, bring my baby back. Obviously, I knew they couldn't but that's all I needed at that time, there wasn't anything else. I didn't need somebody saying it'll be okay in time; time is a healer or something along those lines. All I needed was my baby, why didn't people just get that?

So soon, Jas was back to work and I was all alone at home. He would call quite often just to check how I was during the day. Sometimes I'd be crying, and he felt helpless, as he was at work. The first few days and particularly the day he returned to work, people were asking him how's I was, they were not checking how he was although he had also lost his son. The bereavement midwife had warned us that people would ask about me more so than him and it became very apparent, that would indeed be the case.

Then one day I got a text message from my aunt, she'd heard that morning that Gary Barlow's daughter was stillborn and she wanted to check that how I was and whether I'd be okay about this as it was obviously all over the news. I felt heartbroken for them. I also wondered if this might help break the stigma of baby loss because I'd already learned that there was a big taboo about talking about baby loss. Although I'd know it'd happened in the past to other celebrities like Amanda Holden I just felt maybe Gary Barlow would do something to break the silence on this. I felt for them so much I knew that they would be struggling in the first initial dark period and that it lasts for a long time unfortunately. If I remember correctly, Gary Barlow was doing X Factor at this time and I knew the live shows would be starting a month after. I felt for him I wondered if he would he pull out during this time of grieving or whether he would put on a mask which so many of us do and carry on with his job, and then take that mask off after he's been on the TV. This is a terribly brave thing to do.

It is a strange world we live in, where we can't show our own emotions and where if ever we talk about a baby we've lost, it brings an awkwardness to everybody else. Why do we do that to ourselves? It's not good for our mental health is it? Unfortunately, that's all about breaking the silence isn't it, something that has been tried for so long but never really succeeded. It feels like we can only really talk about baby loss with people that have also lost a baby. What people need to know is, just saying are you ok, can I do anything for you is fine, but they don't need to make it awkward. They need to appreciate the fact that they have spoken about your loss, rather than cross the street to avoid you.

In August, a few things happened; one was that party that I told you about that we didn't go to regardless of the relentless pressure from Jas's mum. I didn't tell her the mother of the little boy didn't want us there anyway. Then we found out that one of Jas's close friends, had given birth to a baby boy and didn't even text Jas to tell him the good news. You can take that in two different ways of course, either he felt guilty and didn't want to share the news with Jas, or that he didn't want to put a dampener on their special time. Jas took this quite hard, as ordinarily his friend would have texted him immediately. It felt like we were in our own sort of bubble, that nobody felt they could talk to us and tell us any good news. We are the type of people however, that always like to hear good news from others and are always happy for others. Then suddenly we were being pushed away like we were aliens and only wanted people to talk to us about bad stuff. One of my cousins also got married that month. The one who'd sent the inappropriate wedding invitation, just as our son had passed away. We didn't attend obviously; however the rest of my family did need to go. I knew really they didn't want to be celebrating anything as they were still in their grieving modes, but our society finds ways to shame you if you don't attend an event without good reason. So, they put on their best smiles and carried on. They were still obviously happy for my cousin as we all were, it was just that nobody was in a party mood.

Around this time, I had to go for my six-week check-up with the midwife at the doctor's surgery. I walked in and she had a big smile on her face. She said she was surprised I'd not brought the baby with me. I stopped in my tracks. I couldn't believe they had still not updated my records to say that I had a stillborn. I had to tell her. Her smile quickly faded away and she said how sorry she was and that she would update the records immediately. She examined me and said that I'd healed perfectly fine and that she was sorry again for not knowing. I replied saying it wasn't her fault. As I walked outside, I bumped into somebody that's known by the family, somebody I don't know very well. She asked me how I was doing and gave me a hug. I said I was as well as I could be, and she replied in a chirpy voice saying that I didn't need to worry and that I could have another one as I was still young. I looked at her like thinking 'what did you just say, I can have another one don't worry,' like this is nothing. I was fuming I've had to get away from her. I said goodbye to her and just walked away. In the car I was just so angry, and I was thinking, 'well you have two children, what if one of them died and somebody said to you, well it's okay at least you have another one, would that make it okay!' How dare she say that to me. It was shocking how insensitive somebody could be. When Jas arrived home from work, I told him what happened and he was fuming too, and said you know what we will hear insensitive comments from people that has become clear already, we're just going to have to control our feelings around it. I said well I wanted to scream at her actually and say, what if one of your children died? It was just so frustrating that I couldn't bring myself to shout back at these people. If I did obviously I would cause a scene and what would society think about that, goodness me. I needed to keep this stiff upper lip, as they say.

I found myself getting deeper and deeper into a dark place. The pain, the emptiness, the sheer horror, tugging at my heart. I needed to be with my boy. I still had my post pregnancy body and no baby to show for it. The excruciating pain of the emptiness was killing me, and during this dark time I could not think of anything else apart from being with Luca. There was only one obvious way that I could be with Luca and that was to take my own life. So, I began to think about what the easiest way for me to take my own life would be. I thought about what would be the quickest most pain-free. Now that I had decided on the way, I needed to go get the material for it. I wasn't thinking of anything else. When you plan to take your own life, it's like you're on a very narrow lane, there's nothing else that you think of apart from that, and for me it was about seeing Luca again. I picked up my car keys ready to leave the house to get the materials that I needed, I looked at the time and thought 'yes soon I'll be with my son.' Then I realised I didn't have long before Jas would be home from work. Oh my gosh Jas, he would be the one to find my body and I began to cry. I realised I couldn't do that to him. He was already grieving; I couldn't let him be the one to find my body. What would that do to him. This stopped me in my tracks. I'd been so hellbent on taking my own life, but I hadn't even thought of what it would do to my husband. It wasn't until I looked at the time of when he'd be coming home that I even gave him any consideration. Thankfully I did though, and it was that, which made me stop the thoughts about taking my own life. I cried for hours, thinking about what I had been about to do. I hadn't thought of anybody else, only my biggest, strongest desire to be with Luca, not all the devastation that I would leave behind. I can see how people do take their own lives, when that pain is so deep, and you are just thinking about ending that horrid pain and that there's no other way. I totally understood, but for me, I was lucky I thought of Jas. It's clear that when other people have taken their own life they haven't thought of the devastation that they're going to leave behind; they can only think about easing their pain or rather ending that pain. I suppose now that I know that feeling, my advice to anybody that would ever want to take their own life like I did, would be to please think about the person who's going to find your body, and the aftermath and devastation that you will leave behind.

I realised at this moment that I needed help when Jas arrived home. He could see that I had been crying a lot, as my eyes were puffy and red. He asked what was the matter as I can see you been crying a lot today, what has been different today? I told him that I'd thought about taking my own life, because I couldn't stand the pain, the emptiness of not having Luca, but that it had been thinking about him finding my body, that had stopped me. He held me so close asking me to promise that I would never ever do anything like that, he said he could not live if I was not here. He told me that he only lived for me now so please, do not ever think of that again. I cried and told him that he was right, I couldn't do that to him, because I loved him too much. Jas messaged his manager that evening to say that I was in a bad way and that he needed to work from home for a few days. His manager agreed and I knew deep inside, he was making sure he was here in case I got those thoughts again.

I did reach out for help. At the hospital when Luca died, we were given this big pack of information. There was information in there about the organisation SANDS (Stillbirth and Neonatal Death support). They had online help. I wasn't ready to talk to people face to face, so I went online and typed my first message and said I'd lost my son who was stillborn at 36 weeks just a few weeks ago and I was struggling. I wrote that I felt so empty, useless, and guilty and felt like my body had failed my son. I got lots of responses, all from ladies that had experienced similar things and they said that they'd also felt the same, over the past few months. Some asked if he'd had a post-mortem and if we'd had the results as yet. I told them we'd not had the results as yet, but I did know that there had been nothing wrong with the placenta and that the paediatrician had said that everything was fine with Luca. One lady came back and said that the post-mortem would give me the answers and that I should hang in there. I knew that's what I had to do, hang in there, and that there was nothing I could do but that. That week we also went to pick up Luca's ashes. To my horror his ashes were in a simply little square cardboard box. I said I wouldn't take them like that and that he should be in an appropriate container. We chose a tube with a picture of a teddy bear on it. The following week we had the letter come through to say that the post-mortem results were in and that we had an appointment to go and speak to an obstetrician at the hospital on the 22 August.

We had decided to scatter Luca's ashes in a river in Leicestershire and strangely enough we had planned it for the 22 August. In Indian tradition scattering the ashes in water means that you are setting them free. This is all I'd ever known about what to do with the ashes so that's what we'd decided to do, but since, I've regretted that decision.

The date couldn't come soon enough for us, whilst waiting for that date lots of thought kept going through my head about what they might say was the cause of Luca's death: they might tell me it was my fault, they might tell me there was something wrong with Luca, maybe there was a genetical fault that caused his death that we could not have known of, nor stopped. I guess in my head I was thinking that one of these reasons might give me some closure and that this might help me move on in some way. The best way for that would be to hear that there was nothing that could have been done and that even if he had lived he would not have survived. That kind of closure was the only thing I could think of which would give me some relief from this endless pain and guilt that I was feeling.

When we sat in the office with this doctor she asked us how we were. Obviously we weren't in a good place, so we said that Jas was back at work and that I was still struggling and feeling a lot of emptiness. I wasn't going to lie, that was the truth. She began asking me about how I felt during my pregnancy. I told her it'd been great, that I had barely had any morning sickness and it was a textbook pregnancy. There was nothing that I could pinpoint that I could have done wrong. She looked at me and told me I hadn't done anything wrong. She mentioned that I'd had the diabetes check and that was all fine and that all my other checks were fine too. Jas mentioned that we had been to the hospital a week before for what we thought was leaking water and she said she'd seen the notes about that where they'd marked down that everything was okay. I asked if something had been missed. She looked through the charts and then became concerned and encircled a chart from the day we had our growth scan at 24 weeks. She asked if anybody had followed up on this and we said no and what did that mean, why should it have been followed up? She said the chart showed that Luca was small for his gestation period. I said I didn't understand as we had been told that everything was fine that day. She pointed to the chart and showed us the line that indicated he was on the smaller side for his abdominal measurement and told us that this is something that would normally be followed up. She explained however, that there was nothing from the post- mortem which had found anything wrong with Luca, he was perfectly formed. The only thing they could put his death was down to an IUGR which stands for Intrauterine Growth Restriction. She said if this had been picked up then they could have monitored it. When I heard those words right there, it made me wonder, does that mean my son should be here? That just took my breath away; I couldn't comprehend the words that were coming out of her mouth. After that, the conversation became a blur, I couldn't focus on anything else apart from her saying that it should have been followed up.

After the meeting we went back home, Jas and I were just so confused. We had been told everything was fine, how could they miss that Luca was small? It seemed like a very significant thing that had been missed. The person had been so busy talking about the man that lived in our house before. Perhaps she didn't do her job correctly that day because she was so consumed with talking about other things, that were completely irrelevant. It didn't escape me that it had been Friday the 13th of April. I I will always remember it as the day that my son's growth scan was incorrectly read. I will always hate Friday the 13th from now on. I asked Jas if that meant Luca should be here. He replied that he didn't know and that although she hadn't really said that in as many words, reading between the lines, perhaps yes.

"So, were they negligent?" I shouted.

Jas explained that we couldn't know that for sure but based on what she's told us and the fact that it wasn't followed up, it sounded like it could be negligence. I thought about the possibility, that my baby wasn't here because some woman hadn't done her job right and had kept talking about stupid stuff, and that this might have cost us our son's life. I shouted, I cried Jas held me. He was obviously as frustrated as me and was trying to take it all in himself too.

So, I didn't get that closure that I thought I would, or should I say I'd been hoping for. Instead, my head was spinning with the thought of someone having missed a very vital part of his growth chart and that there was a chance that our son could have been here. This was the opposite of what I thought I'd be coming out of that meeting with. I don't think there's any words that can actually really explain what was going through my head at that time. What I wanted to do was find that woman and show her the chart and scream at her that it was because of her that my son wasn't here. I was processing this information and I'd have to replay it over and over again in my head to really understand what had been said, and discuss it with Jas, this was no time for hasty action.

We decided to go ahead and do what we'd said we were going to do that day, set our baby free. For the rest of the day, we focused on that. We made our way to Leicestershire with his ashes in the little teddy bear tube. It costs a hundred pounds to spread ashes at this river. It was a beautiful day, so, I'd decided I would take some flowers from the garden and scatter them with his ashes in the water so that he had something from home.

We arrived at the front office, which was a part of a cafe really, and explained we had booked to scatter ashes today. Initially, the gentleman seemed shocked to see us but then said that he knew I was Sharon. I replied yes and explained that my companion was my husband Jas. He took us towards the boat that we were going to be using that day and introduced us to the driver who explained that he'd take us to a quiet part of the river where we could then do what we came for today. We said thank you and got onto the boat. As we went along, we looked at the scenery around us. It was very peaceful. There were other people on their boats, some summer paddle boats and others just enjoying the sunny weather. We came to a spot up river which was so quiet you couldn't hear anything. The driver told us he'd stop there, and we could have as much time as we needed. We got the ashes out; at that moment my hands became shaky. It was time again to say goodbye but significantly, this was the final time to say goodbye because this was the last thing we had to do. There would be no more holding him after this. I began to cry and so did Jas. I wanted to make sure that we dropped the flowers at the same time as the ashes, so I was trying to hold both things at once. Jas and I both had our hands on this tube of ashes with its cute teddy bear design on the front. We spoke to him first after taking off the lid.

I said, "this is the final part son, we won't get to hold you again after this, until we meet again in heaven. Please float away, be free rest in peace, we will love you and miss you forever with every beat of our hearts for the rest of our lives. You will always be our firstborn and so much wanted, our beloved son."

Jas began slowly releasing his ashes into the water and I was dropping the flowers in at the same time, they were something from home for him to go with. We sobbed so much as we did it that our hands were shaking, and we kept whispering about loving Luca and cried so much. When the tube was empty, we watched as the ashes started floating away with the flowers from home. The water was shining from the sun rays above. I thought God was shining down on us right then as we were saying those final goodbyes. It was lovely that the sun was shining. I love the summer and sunshine, it helped make that day right for me.

After a short while, I gestured to the driver that we were ready to go back. He turned the boat around and off we went. I looked back and saw the flowers floating away. We sat for a while back at the café, had an ice cream and watched the river and then we tried to pay the owner. He wouldn't take our money. It was then I realised why he had looked shocked earlier. It was because he had noticed the teddy bear tube and realised that the ashes were of a child. We insisted on paying him something, but he said no, he wouldn't take our money and he wished us well on our journey. We thanked him and he shook Jas's hand and gave me a pat on the shoulder as if to say, ' I feel for you.'

On the way home we spoke about how perfect the day was in terms of weather and being able to do this for Luca but in the back of our minds we were still thinking about what we'd heard at the meeting that day. We couldn't get that out of our heads, but I think we were both just too exhausted by then to keep going over it in our heads. When we got home, neither of us were very hungry so we had a light bite, watched some TV and then I went to bed. The next day Jas worked from home I got up late, having had a lie in.

A week or so later there was an article in I think it was the Daily Mail, about a couple that had been through a similar thing to us in a hospital down south. They had been taking legal action and it was found that negligence was involved and that was the reason their child was stillborn. Jas sent it to me via a link on WhatsApp. His message said it seemed like a similar story to ours. I agreed with. The article had the name of the solicitors the couple had used, so I suggested to Jas that I could call them. We agreed to discuss it later when he was home. Dinner was always made by the time he came home, and I'd made something light as it'd been quite a warm day. We sat down and talked about whether I should call these solicitors and explain what had happened with us. He'd been thinking about it during the day and thought we should. He felt we owed it to Luca. I said I'd ring the next day.

The following day I called the solicitors and spoke to the lady that had dealt with the case that was in the paper. She asked me questions and decided it was very similar to the case in the paper. She agreed to take our case on a no win no fee basis as we had no money to take it to court ourselves. She then asked for all the hospital details, so that she could request medical records of my pregnancy. We knew this was the start of the legal case could start but what we didn't know then was how long time it would take before we would get an answer.

Summary.

On reflecting back at this stage, it's clear to see that when you think you're doing everything right you are often not thinking straight enough to understand that later, you would have done things in a different way.

For example, when I said that I would later regret scattering Luca's ashes, it was because I found out that actually you can make jewellery out of ashes and if I had known that, I would have had them made into something I could wear so that he would be with me every day. Alternatively, there are also glass ornaments that can be made with the ashes inside too, something beautiful to keep in the home.

Also, a lot of pressure comes from other people and it's fair to say you need to stand your own ground if you don't want to do something. Don't do it no matter what other people are saying, go by how you and your partner feel.

Obviously, life carried on for others, whilst I was still in the deepness of grief and in a very dark place. I wouldn't want anyone to feel like this, I wouldn't wish it on my worst enemy. The fact is life goes on for everyone else around you and I'm happy for them that it does. What becomes clear over the weeks after of losing your child, is that you see the people that are really truly there for you. Steven my brother had been an immense support for both of us, and it was at this time that Jas said he's not just my brother in law he is my brother. The difference it made for Jas to have Steven's support was clear in those words. It's important that the fathers also get as much support as they can from their friends and relatives because they are finding it hard to be strong for you the grieving mother. My husband knew that it was ten times harder for me I was the one that had given birth to Luca, he had grown in my womb and I had a bond with him way before Jas could feel his kicks. This is important to remember for fathers out there supporting a grieving partner. She has been through so much more physically, emotionally and mentally, because childbirth takes it out of a woman, and it is a hundred times worse when it is a stillborn. It is important though that you take care of your own mental health, so that you can be there for your wife too.

You'll start seeing the true colours of people around you in the first few weeks, shocking things will be said, things that you can never imagine people would ever think, let alone say. Trust me, it is hard to bite your tongue and not shout back at these people. This is the hardest time saying all those parts of the goodbyes to your baby, but when that part is done it doesn't get easier, it just becomes different. You will find your new normal, but it takes time.

For those supporting the couple who have just lost their baby, please do the simple things that will help them. They won't be in the mood to cook, so make them some simple meals, nothing heavy as often they would have lost most of their appetite. Offer to do shopping for them, maybe mundane tasks like ironing or cleaning. Those first eight to ten weeks are so important, whilst you still get on with your life, please also keep checking in on the couple too.

For other people that are not close enough to do the above, please do not treat the couple like lepers. Don't keep your distance, and then turn up in their lives when you think they are over it. Understand that a couple will never be over the loss of their child, just like you would never be. If you cannot understand their feeling, try closing your eyes and imagining that someone has told you that your child has died. Your heart will hurt immediately just by trying to imagine it and your eyes will fill with tears. You won't want to imagine the worse thing ever happening to you… But remember this is this couple's new reality.

The couple will be a new version of themselves, don't look for the old them… that part of them & part of their heart died with their baby. They are now living a new normal and finding their feet slowly again.

Chapter Three
Anxieties

Now that we knew that there was nothing wrong with Luca, we were given the all-clear to start trying for another baby if we so wished. Jas and I had discussed whether we wanted to do this now or give it some time. I knew that I was a mum without her baby and my arms were aching with the emptiness of not being able to hold my child. I also knew that having another child would not replace Luca, but that it would help to fill the absolute horrific void in my life. I was a mother without a child here to show that I was a mother.

Obviously one of the things that was needed for me to be able to have another child, was for me to be ovulating. My menstrual cycle had not come back at all since giving birth to Luca. It would be fair to say that the grief, the stress, and everything else that goes with having lost a child, played a significant part in this.

At this point I was using the SANDS online support site quite a lot. I'd spoken to bereaved mothers and asked them for their thoughts on when the right time is to try and have another baby. Clearly everyone is different and that is exactly the response I got. They were all very empathetic of course but it was clearly a decision that had to be right for us. One woman had said to me that there would never be a right time and the longer you wait the more anxious you might get about it, but that if you do it straight away, you would still be anxious about it anyway. Let's face it, a subsequent pregnancy was not going to be easy and would be filled with anxiety, no matter how long or not we left it. We were both parents without their child here and we wanted nothing more than to be parents to a living child. We gave it a lot of thought and came to the same conclusion. We decided that once my menstrual cycle returned, we would start trying for baby.

A couple of weeks earlier my aunt and sister had asked me to join them to go to a theme park with their children. It was another way of them trying to get me out the house as well. I took them up on the offer and Jas told me he thought it might be good for me to go out with the children as they always make me laugh. I did have some good laughs with them but whilst we were out, I noticed so many mothers with pushchairs and small babies I had to try my hardest all day not to cry. I didn't want to ruin the day out for the children. This made me realise just how much I really did need to have a baby again.

Meanwhile my mum said it would be good for us to get away and have a change of scenery somewhere that no one knew what had happened to us. She suggested we could perhaps go for a city break in Europe. She offered to pay for it and told us not to worry about the finances. We decided as we had always wanted to go to Rome that we would go there. Making all the arrangements gave me something to do and something to sort of look forward to really. In the second week of September we headed off to Rome. It was nice actually, quite hot on some days. We were staying near the centre, so we could walk to bars, restaurants, and other sites apart from Vatican City. That was the only place that was too far for us to walk to but that we had figured out a way to get there.

We'd arrived in Rome not too late in the evening, but it was dark, as our bus had been delayed on arrival. That was our prepaid transfer. We got checked in, got into the room, put our cases in and headed straight out for something to eat as we were starving. There were lots of restaurants and bars on the street we're staying on, so we'd decided to just take a walk up the road and see where looked good to eat. We'd said we'd have a couple of drinks and then get our heads down, ready for some sightseeing the next day. We ended up in an Irish bar where there was music playing. It was a really warm evening, so we sat outside. I watched the locals going by. We had a nice dinner, something quite simple, I think it was burger and chips if I remember correctly. The atmosphere on the street was great, we knew we had picked the right place.

The next morning, we woke up and had breakfast which was included in our booking. We filled our stomachs and then went off for some sightseeing. We had a map so we knew where to go, but don't ask me to recall the names of everywhere we went, as I really wouldn't remember. What I did notice massively was that wherever we were walking along to, I would see Luca's name. Luca is an Italian name and I had not expected nor even thought about it actually, but whatever street we would go down or maybe it was just a coincidence for me, but his name was mentioned on so many places. It was just everywhere. It was quite comforting. It made me feel like he was on the trip with us and everywhere we turned there it was, his name Luca, right in front of us.

When we went down to the Spanish Steps and looked at the views, it was stunning. On our way down to the Trevi fountain, there was a little square with a bistro and little shop, it was very quiet. The square was called Saint Luca Square. I was just astonished. I took a photo and just smiled. Jas saw me looking up and looked up towards what I was seeing. He put his arm around me as if to say, 'yeah that's our boy.' By the Trevi fountain it was really busy and everyone was taking photos trying to get the best shot. It was so idyllic, and I found a spot to sit down and Jas took my photo. They say that if you throw a coin in the fountain and make a wish, it comes true. Well just try and guess what I was wishing for, yep I was wishing for that my menstrual cycle would come back so that we could try for a baby again. Never in a million years would I ever have thought I would be wishing to have my period, but Oh yes, that was what I needed now, so that I could ovulate and try to have a pregnancy. At this point I was only thinking of getting pregnant, not so much baby, but pregnancy was the first step of course.

We were in Rome for three nights. One night we had a delicious meal at an Italian restaurant up the road from our hotel. It was so lovely that I wanted to go back there the next day, but it was full. On this day we had been to the Colosseum and the ruins next to it across the road. That had taken us a whole day, so luckily we had done the Spanish Steps and the fountain the day, before knowing that on our final day we would be going to Vatican City.

On the third day, we woke up knowing that we needed to head out early, as the Vatican City would get full very quickly. We asked the hotel reception how to get to the Metro and they told us which stop to take, so we knew where we were going, and it was straight forward. When we got off the Metro and started walking towards Vatican City, there were people selling audio tours. We thought this would be a good idea as there's so much history there and just looking at it wasn't going to be enough. We wanted to hear about it too. We had heard that we would bump into people like this along the way from friends that had been before so it took us by no surprise and we knew we would get to queue jump if we were part of an audio tour, so we did exactly that. It was fantastic as we walked down towards Vatican City and saw it in the distance, it was just amazing. The group wasn't very big, I think there was only about 10 of us. Once we got there though it was so busy. As we were jumping the queues, I looked at Jas and laughed, we'd definitely done the right thing by being part of a tour. Being a Christian, this was definitely one place I had always wanted to come and finally I was here as we were looking around. The other places I want to go one day are Jerusalem and Bethlehem. I was just amazed at what I was looking at and heard on the audio and I was taking photos, it was just magical. Before you go into the Sistine Chapel there's a little shop where you can buy memorabilia. I saw some beautiful prayer beads that looked like pearl and silver entwined, and I purchased these along with a few other bits.

I felt so at peace and at ease there, like there was an inner peace within myself. It was the type of feeling I normally only got at the Coventry Cathedral. Although there were lots of people there, they didn't block any of this inner peace that I was receiving. The place was magical. I sat down in one of the corners which was quieter and away from lots of the loud people taking lots of photos. I say loud but they were just tourists talking to each other, trying to be heard amongst all the mass of people there. I was tucked away in this nice little corner watching as I was looking around, staying quiet. I prayed that we would welcome a child next year before Luca's anniversary and that the child would be completely healthy with no problems, and that I would be too.

Soon after we left Vatican City and made our way back to our hotel. We sat down, had a cup of tea freshened up with showers, and then headed out for dinner. The restaurant I had wanted to go to as I mentioned earlier was full, so we had to look for somewhere else. We walked around for a little while and then we settled on a little bistro on a side street. I had a pizza and a glass of wine and Jas had steak and beer. When the food came out, I wasn't too keen on the pizza I can't quite remember why, but I remember I didn't enjoy it very much. Jas said however it was the best steak he had ever had. At least one of us was happy. I made up for it with the dessert though.

The next day our pickup was early. So, we'd packed our bags the night before when we'd got back to the hotel and gone to sleep in good time ready for an early start the next day. We arrived home early afternoon. It was nice to get back and the sun was shining. Jas still had another day off, and we just chilled out at home, watching TV and had a takeaway.

About ten days later guess what, my menstrual cycle appeared, I was delighted as was Jas. At this time though I wasn't going to put all my hope's into conceiving straight away as it had taken us 4 months with Luca. I was also studying for my Prince 2 certificate in project management. It was good that I had some focus, it was what I needed at this time, so that I didn't go insane with the thought of trying to conceive. A few weeks later, I was in a classroom surrounded by people all studying for their Prince 2 qualification, it was a crash course over four and a half days. I was surprised to see that my sister in law's aunt was on the same course. It was a nice surprise to see someone there that I knew. However, I hadn't seen her since Luca had died so our initial conversation in our first break was about Luca. We stood to one side of the room because obviously there was going to be tears.

I worked hard that week and really applied myself. I wanted to pass and finally have my certificate as a project manager. This was the same week that I ovulated too however and strangely it was on the day that I had no homework. I laugh about it now as it was definitely important at that time. I had passed the first part of the project management course which was the Foundation and now I had to sit the exam for Practitioner on the Friday morning. It was quite intense, but I got through it and my course was finished. I wouldn't get the results for two weeks but that was fine. I had finished the course and had given it my all. I had passed my Foundation and if I did pass the Practitioner level too, then I had done a bloody good job. As a grieving mum trying to study whilst thinking about conceiving and everything else that was going on in my head, I thought it would be a miracle if I actually passed the Practitioner.

So, the following week I just chilled and didn't really do a lot. I think I was mentally exhausted from all the time and energy I had put into the course. In my head I knew that this coming weekend would be ten days from the day I had ovulated, and I could take a pregnancy test. Yes, that's right, I'm one of those people that start to count from the day she ovulates, and I knew ten days was the earliest time you can take a pregnancy test. I'd done it with Luca, and I was going to do it the same way now. That Sunday morning it'd been a whole week of waiting and I woke up and I took the test. I didn't tell Jas I was going to do this. It was enough pressure for me, and I didn't want to put it on him as well. So, I brushed my teeth, and had a wash whilst waiting for the test results to appear on the screen. I dried myself off and I went over to have a look. Wow I was pregnant, and this was the first time we'd tried. I was pregnant, I was giddy but crying as well at the same time knowing that there was going to be a long journey ahead of us.

I picked up the test and went downstairs. Jas was watching cricket. I sat next to him and handed him the test. He looked at me and his eyes filled up with tears immediately. We just held each other and cried happy tears. I suggested that we didn't tell anybody for now, just Jas and I would know, and I would call the midwife the next day and make an appointment. We knew this time around things were going to be really hard, but we also knew what to look out for too and that no one and I mean no one was going to brush us off with saying everything's fine, because this time I would want everything explained thoroughly.

Around this time 'Rihanna' released her song 'Diamonds.' I loved it immediately and started changing the words.

Suddenly I would be singing in my head:-

"'Shine bright, tonight, Luca...you're beautiful, my diamond in the sky." That's how I saw Luca now, my diamond in the sky.

"I find a light in the beautiful sky, then I am happy, you are my little diamond in the sky,

You're a shooting star I see, a vision of my son I see, if I could hold you, I'd feel alive, you're my diamond in the sky.

I knew at once you were my beautiful babe, my beautiful babe,

So, shine bright tonight, Luca, you're beautiful my diamond in the sky, I'll love you, forever, You're beautiful my diamond in the sky."

This has been my song ever since, and it's my ringtone on my phone too.

Jas had already decided he was going to watch football with some friends at the pub that afternoon. I can't remember who was playing but it must have been Manchester United that's the only time he would ever go out or watch football with his friends, because a lot of them were United fans and they liked to get together for those matches.

He'd popped in to see his folks on the way there and they'd been talking to him about building a shed at the back of our garden. Now I mean, not an ordinary shed, a brick built shed, an outhouse really. Jas being a sort of 'yeah yeah' type of guy, he doesn't really listen or take in what's actually being said sometimes so they took this as an agreement. Now, this shed was to be built by his brother in law who was just starting out as a builder and had just a few people working for him. However, Jas's parents wanted to pay for it and that obviously was very generous of them. With Jas's 'yeah yeah' type of approach the next thing I knew was that his dad and his brother in law were at our house measuring the back of the garden to see how big this shed can be. I was a bit surprised and taken aback by what was going on and asked what they were doing as we didn't even need a shed. They said that it was already agreed and it was as if my opinion didn't count for anything even though it was my house too for goodness sake. They measured all the way across the full back of the garden. I told them we didn't need a big shed; we had nothing to put in it. They suggested we'd soon start using it like they do there's. Jas's mum makes food in it, like curries and things. I told them I wasn't the type of person that made big pots of curry in a shed and I most certainly didn't need a shed going across the whole of my garden. It makes me laugh now thinking back on it. I asked them to just make a small shed and said we would never have enough to put anything in it. I wasn't completely against the idea; I was just surprised at how quickly they came to measure it up.

I called Jas and asked him if he knew what had just happened. As I explained, he laughed and said he hadn't actually agreed to it, he'd just said yeah yeah, maybe. Well your 'yeah yeah' as usual, has now been taken as a full on yes I told him. Oh, I was so annoyed at him that he'd not told them to just leave it for now and wait until he's discussed it with me. I suppose in his defence he was thinking about the fact that we'd had a positive pregnancy test that morning and everything else that anybody was saying to him was just going in one ear and out the other. I was thinking well I've had a positive pregnancy test this morning and now I want to take things easy and let things glide with ease, no stress no pressure or anything. Oh, how little had I known that was about to be challenged.

The next morning Jas's brother in law and his team of three people knocked on the door and told me they were here to build our shed/outbuilding. I was just gobsmacked, I thought I was in a nightmare and was thinking, are you seriously starting this nonsense right now? I couldn't believe it, what a way to start my new pregnancy. Obviously, my hormones were having a big part in my reaction here. I just didn't need this right now. I just wanted Jas to have the guts to tell them to leave it as we didn't want it, we had other things to think about, but it was too late, they were already starting to dig out the foundations. It took about three weeks to build. In between I'd had an appointment with the midwife, and she was delighted to hear that we were pregnant again. She explained how we would be carefully monitored and that she would immediately write to the hospital and assign me an obstetrician. In these three weeks, instead of resting and taking it easy as I had wanted to, I was constantly making teas and sometimes food for the builders outside. I was having to put up with dirt and noise, and waking up early, to let people in and out of my house to use the facilities. It was not the best start to my pregnancy and let's not forget, I was still grieving as well. Just because I had a positive pregnancy test, it did not mean that I had suddenly stopped grieving for Luca and nor would I ever. The following week I got a letter through the post saying that I had passed my Prince 2 Practitioner Exam. I was delighted. I had not really expected to pass, considering everything that was still going on. This was good news. I called Jas at work and told him immediately. He was delighted for me as he knew I had put so much work into this, and at such a difficult and dark time of our lives too.

The week after that was Diwali, the festival of lights for many Indian religions. This was something I hadn't really celebrated massively in the past, as I am Christian, and Jas doesn't really pay too much attention to it either. I would however, always leave a light on at night as my aunt had told me too many years ago. Regardless of whether we did or not, we were still in a very dark place grieving for our son and we had no desire to celebrate anything not even Christmas, not anything. I received a message whilst Jas was out getting a takeaway from the mother of the little baby that was born five days after Luca. I'll actually refer to them as the couple now. She asked what we were doing for Diwali celebrations which came as a surprise as she had never in the previous years ever asked me this, I felt she was doing it on purpose. I explained we had no desire to be celebrating anything at this time as we were still grieving for our son. I was very polite and clear. She responded extremely abruptly and told me to get over it and, it's not her sons' fault that our son had died. I was shocked and horrified to my core at her words. I was crying by the time Jas came home. He asked me what was wrong, and I showed him my phone and the messages that I had received. He was livid he could not believe that somebody would even think these words, let alone say them or type them with such clarity and malice. She was clearly trying to hurt somebody who was already hurting so much. I can't quite remember what happened at this point, I think he texted her back from my phone saying to leave his wife alone or he texted her husband to tell him to ask his your wife to stop texting me as she was upsetting me deeply. It was certainly one or the other. This bugged Jas for so many days after this. On the weekend he took my phone to show his cousin the messages and asked if we were overreacting. His cousin was shocked at the audacity that somebody could even send such messages and be so insensitive when she had a child the same age as ours and he was living a fine life here. We had not done anything, or said anything in the sense of being nasty to them for having a living child, but the two of them had carried on for months now digging away at us and saying nasty things about our son who had died. The following month even more sniping came from the male of the couple. He told Jas that he was too sensitive because he would not attend a party for a cousin's daughter who had turned eighteen. This time it caused a huge argument and it was clear that he would never speak to them again.

That aside, we had managed to get an appointment with the obstetrician that had given us the post-mortem results. She was delighted that we were pregnant and assured us again that we would be treated as high risk and would be taken care of. We would have appointments with her very regularly. First she wanted to have a little look inside and make sure there was a heartbeat. As I was literally in the early weeks of pregnancy this was an internal examination as opposed to an external scan. After seeing the little heartbeat on the screen and receiving confirmation that yes there was a little baby growing inside of me the obstetrician told us that when we got to twelve weeks, she would put us on aspirin. She told us this was just to make sure that my blood stayed thin enough to feed my baby throughout my pregnancy. This was obviously the first stage of eliminating anything bad happening which could mean losing the baby. We saw her again around ten weeks pregnancy. She did a scan, and everything was good, and then we had our official twelve-week scan after that. Needless to say, we were in and out of the hospital maternity unit for the entire pregnancy. There were many appointments with long waiting times but all I could think about was will my baby be alive at the end of this.

We still hadn't told anybody that we were pregnant even after the twelve-week scan. We just wanted to go as long as we could without even having to mention it. Just before the twelve-week scan we had Christmas and New Year. I didn't even put the Christmas Tree up as I had no joyous feelings for Christmas this year. It wasn't the Christmas that I had planned it to be. There were no little baby gifts under the tree or in a stocking with Luca's name on. I couldn't bring myself to celebrate, so I just didn't put the tree up. I just wanted to hibernate this Christmas and not see anybody. My mum insisted that it would do is better to be with the family and that none of us were really going to enjoy this Christmas as much as we should have been, but she thought it would be nice if we at least had Christmas dinner together. Jas and I decided we would only go for Christmas dinner as the whole day was just awful. I had bought Jas an Everton shirt as that is the team he supports. This is something I had already planned before Luca had died. It was going to be his gift to his dad on his first Christmas and the Everton shirt would have Luca written on the back and his birth date. I still did all that.

On the gift card I wrote, 'to my daddy even though I'm not here with you this present is something mummy had already thought of before I died, and I still want you to have it because I still live on in your heart .' Jas cried when he saw it and read the message. It was just something I needed to do to remember Luca at Christmas, just for us two.

Jas went to his parents to give a few gifts to his family, but I didn't go. I really wasn't up to it. His mum called me and asked why I hadn't come, and I just burst out crying on the phone, telling her that it wasn't a joyous day for me. I knew that I would have had to pretend to be happy and that I could not face it.

I had agreed to go to my family because I knew I wouldn't have to pretend or hide how I was feeling. I realised that at times like this I behaved quite differently with different people. There were those who I had to pretend to be okay for and the ones that I could actually show my true feelings to. When I did arrive at my parents' home in Leicestershire, I burst into tears as soon as I went through the door. My mum was already crying when we arrived, and I just went into one of the small rooms and cried with my mum and my brother Steven. My sister in law Olivia was in the kitchen peeling some vegetables and she gave me a hug, but Sunny was working abroad again. It was definitely a day of ups and downs. My dad did a speech just before dinner thanking The Lord for this special day, he also mentioned the people that were missing, Sunny because he was abroad and Luca who was in heaven. This again made me cry, so I left the table and had a good cry before I returned. Olivia's parents and sisters joined us for the day, and it sort of broke things up a little because it added a different atmosphere and we could talk about different things. The New Year went by in a blur. I honestly can't remember what we did. I think we were in bed early. I was still feeling quite tired with it being my first trimester.

Time was dragging, as I wanted my pregnancy to fast forward. I still had my post-pregnancy body which was obviously disguising some of the pregnancy in the early stages anyway. We knew there would be a point at which we wouldn't be able to disguise it as a post-pregnancy body any longer and would have to tell people that I was pregnant. Luckily, we managed to get to about sixteen or seventeen weeks before we actually started telling people. We told immediate family only and our very closest friends who I think of as family anyway.

It was now early February 2013 and my mum and dad were being baptised at Coventry Cathedral where they had completed their Alpha course. I wore one of Jas's hoodies to disguise the fact I was pregnant. There was a nice little celebration afterwards in Saint Michaels house next to the cathedral. The food was served and everyone who had taken the time to come, talked merrily. I could tell people were looking at me, but they certainly weren't saying anything, wondering to themselves if I may be pregnant. It just felt it a bit too soon to be telling wider group and I certainly didn't want to say anything on that day because it was about my mum and dad's baptisms.

Within the next couple of weeks, we did start telling wider family and friends. We weren't deliberately calling everyone telling them excitingly that we were pregnant again, because that feeling really wasn't there because we were also so anxious. The innocence of having a normal pregnancy had been taken away from us and the enjoyment certainly wasn't there because in our heads we had gone through this before and at the end our baby had died. So, this time it was a case of confirming that I was pregnant and that we hoped for the best. When people gave their congratulations, I felt like telling them to save their congratulations until the baby was here safe and sound. Obviously it is a natural instinct for people to say congratulations, but for me since Luca had died if ever I've heard that anybody is pregnant I've always said to them that it's great news to hear and I've saved the congratulations until the baby has arrived safely into the world and mother and baby are all well. To my delight whilst calling a few of my cousins to tell them I was pregnant, I found out that my cousin Karen was also pregnant, and she was two months behind me with her baby due in September. This was lovely because we agreed that in a few months we would do some shopping together. We did do that, and it was really nice being pregnant together, because for me it was just somebody else to talk to about the pregnancy. It was also good knowing that our babies were going to be close in age and as we were close as cousins we hoped that they would also be. When Jas told his parents and his sister who was there at the same time, they were so happy, and his sister gave him a big hug. The people who did not pay any attention or say anything about him having another baby were the couple that had been very nasty to us. I guess there was no real surprise there considering their nature.

I bought a Doppler monitor so that I check on the baby's heartbeat at home myself. I knew that there could be times where it might not work straight away and I knew that I wasn't going to let that get to me, but for my peace of mind and for Jas we felt it was something we wanted to do. Jas would work one or two days from home just to check I was okay and just to be with me really for the pregnancy. It had taken longer for me to feel the kicks this time because my body wasn't as slim I was told. I didn't actually start feeling the kicks until I was about nineteen weeks pregnant, with Luca it had been much sooner. We knew by now that we were having a baby boy, when we were told the news by the obstetrician we both cried it felt like déjà vu. This baby boy had a due date that was six days before Luca's. You can imagine how even more anxious that made me, I was feeling this was an extremely like for like pregnancy. I had not had much morning sickness, it all felt so familiar and knowing that the due dates were only six days apart that just blew my mind. I could see the dates appointments were coming up and I was thinking that I'd been here this time last year, with just a few days difference. It really did feel like I was living in Groundhog Day in many ways.

Mother's Day came in March. I cried most of the day and stayed in bed longer. Jas made a card on a website with Luca's picture that I still keep next to my bed to this day.

"You will always be my Mummy and I will always be with you," it read. He signed it "Love you forever, Luca and my little brother Ky."

Just before my twenty-three weeks of pregnancy, Jas was working from home and I was watching This Morning. I hadn't felt the baby kick in a while, so I started to do the things that I did with Luca to get him moving, have a cold drink, eat something sweet, have something fizz. Jas suggested we used the Doppler monitor on which we'd managed to hear the heartbeat plenty of times. He thought he might be just sleeping, and we could reassure ourselves. So, we got out the Doppler monitor and we moved it around, then held it still, then moved it around a bit more. We held it in a place but there was no heartbeat. I was getting a little worked up by now as you can imagine. Jas kept telling me to try and stay calm, but I knew he was a bit worried too. We gave it a bit more time as we knew that the Doppler monitor wasn't always one hundred per cent. Previously we had always found a heartbeat with it however, so, not feeling the movements and not hearing the heartbeat was cause for alarm for us.

We called the hospital. I told them we needed to come in as we couldn't feel the baby moving and they agreed. Jas messaged his manager and explained what was happening and he was very understanding and said yes, we should go to the hospital. On arrival at the reception desk we gave in our papers and sat down to wait. I still hadn't felt him move. One of the triage midwives refused to give us a CTG and said that as I was not over twenty-four weeks they didn't do this. I explained that our son had been stillborn the year before and that we needed reassurance that our baby was okay, she was still very dismissive and not understanding at all. She said she would speak to somebody else and come back to us.

Whilst we were waiting in the seating area by the front desk, our bereavement midwife walked past, and she saw that we were in a bit of a state. She asked what was wrong. We explained that we were having trouble getting seen because we hadn't passed twenty-four weeks and that I hadn't felt the baby kick since this morning. She immediately went inside and spoke to the triage staff, telling them that we needed some reassurance after what we had already been through. Meanwhile Jas was trying to call our obstetricians secretary to see if she was in and could help us. He left a message and was waiting for a call back. The lady who we'd seen previously called us in and wired me up to the CTG scanner. We could see that there was movement even though I couldn't feel it and knew that things were okay; however her manner had really taken me aback and made me quite anxious and nervous. We received a call back from our doctor, whilst I was attached to the CTG monitor. She said we could go up to her office and she'd do a proper scan. This was music to our ears because that is exactly what we needed to do, to see our son on the screen perfectly fine. That is exactly what happened, we could see him and a whole weight lifted off me. He was fine. We were told he was just at the back of the womb which is why we couldn't feel much movement and why we couldn't pick up his heartbeat. She told us that in ten days' time, when I would be twenty-four weeks pregnant, she'd do a growth scan. So, we made an appointment to go back in ten days. Funnily enough this date was also our wedding anniversary, but I didn't care, I just wanted to see my baby on that day and in fact every day. I knew seeing them on that day, our wedding anniversary would seem extra special.

The ten days went by and everything was okay. I was feeling him a bit more regularly, so there was no reason to be alarmed and I was relieved and calm. Jas took half-day a day's leave and we booked to go to the Marco Pierre White restaurant in Birmingham for dinner that evening to celebrate our anniversary. We went to the hospital in the afternoon for our appointment and had our growth scan done by our obstetrician. He was kicking away whilst she was taking his measurements and jotting them down. She then said something with a serious face which I was not ready for, I hadn't thought that this could ever happen again. She told us that the baby was measuring small again and in an almost identical way to Luca. Tears built up in my eyes and she knew having taken us through the post- mortem results, what we would be feeling and thinking at this time. She said in a very serious tone of voice that we should try to get to thirty-one weeks and then she would deliver the baby early and put him in the NICU (Neonatal Intensive care unit).

Jas and I were beside ourselves. We couldn't believe the same thing was happening again. I had that feeling of déjà vu and the tears flooded out. She tried to reassurance us by telling us that she would put us on weekly monitoring with the Baby Wellbeing Department and that they would scan me every week and do a Doppler test which is where they check the blood flow to the baby is actually going through correctly and at a good speed. These were all new things that we were learning now during this pregnancy that we had never have known in our first one. Well why would we, you always take it that the professionals will tell you the right information.

After the appointment, I didn't really want to go for the anniversary meal but given that she had tried to reassure us Jas and I decided to go. So, I put my maternity black lace dress on and we headed to Birmingham for our meal. Needless to say, at our meal all we talked about were all the possible outcomes and what we should be doing now to prepare to get to thirty-one weeks which was just five weeks away. I said one of the first things I needed to do was to get my hospital bag ready and get some first size baby clothes and wash and dry them and pack them with some small nappies. In some ways, I felt like I was in good hands because this time the size issue hadn't been missed and we had a very good chance that everything would go fine.

The following day I went to Coventry Cathedral my special place where I pray and find my inner peace and I wrote down a prayer. These were the words that I wrote which I'll never forget.

"Father in heaven, I pray to you to give me the strength I need to carry on through this pregnancy and have the safe arrival of my little boy. If he needs to come out early, please look after him and please give him all the fighting spirit he needs to survive. If we get past the thirty-one weeks please can he be born at thirty-six weeks and no later than a week before Luca's birthday, because I can't get through Luca's first birthday and anniversary without knowing that this baby is safe in my arms perfectly healthy and that I am a mother to a living child."

The weeks seemed to go by slowly, this already felt like a ten-year pregnancy to me. I was being checked once a week and then twice a week, then three times a week and then everyday in the latter stages so we got past the thirty-one weeks and there had been growth which was great to see. The growth scan was going in the right direction which was fantastic. The only thing that wasn't great was that then my obstetrician wanted me to go full term right up to the forty weeks. I didn't want to do this as I had lost Luca at thirty-six weeks on the first day of my maternity leave so there was absolutely no way I wanted to go to forty weeks. I thought it would be an absolute nightmare for me to go through an extra four weeks not knowing whether my baby was okay or not and whether he was going to come out alive or not.

This started to put me in panic mode and every night after around thirty-three weeks I would actually wake up during the night and wake up the baby to make sure he was still alive. I was going through a lot of anxiety at this stage. I knew I wasn't doing what was good for the baby as I was waking him up when he was asleep at night and I knew this may bite me in the bum when he was born, but for my own sanity I needed to know that he was okay and he was alive. When we told the obstetrician that we wanted him to be born earlier she was adamant that this was not going to happen. She had been an absolute fantastic obstetrician, and this was the only time that we came to loggerheads.

My closest friends, had been a huge support to me through this pregnancy. We'd met up for dinners and they'd been making sure I was getting out and chatting whenever I needed to. But at this point, I was crying on the phone with my friends and saying that the obstetrician wasn't listening to me and that it's was my baby and it should be my choice after what we've been through. I couldn't see why she couldn't understand what this is doing to me mentally.

In the end, I decided to write a letter explaining my thoughts. I told her that we wanted the baby to be delivered early and we would sign any papers to say that we understood the risks we are taking by asking for him to be born early. I was thirty-four weeks pregnant when I wrote this letter and sent it to our obstetrician. Upon reading the details, she still stood by the fact that she wanted us to go full term. I'd told her in the letter that if she could one hundred percent guarantee that my son would arrive safe, healthy and alive and that I would be okay too, then we would go by her guidance however if there was no guarantee then they would need to follow our instructions. I also made it clear that we were the ones that were living with the grief and the trauma of what had happened to us because of losing Luca and it was our decision as the parents that we would not put our baby in danger. We knew and had heard of babies being born much earlier than this gestation and that they had been perfectly fine and survived and been perfectly healthy in every way. We ended the letter by saying that if she is still not in agreement with us that we would like it to go to her superior and that we would discuss all the options with the head of the department.

This is what happened, the letter went to the head of the Department of Obstetricians at our hospital and a meeting was then scheduled for us to meet. Unfortunately, the first one was cancelled but it was rearranged within a couple of days. You can imagine how anxious we were at this point. At this appointment I was a bit of a mess to be fair and whilst describing my reasoning as to why I needed my baby to be delivered early I couldn't really control myself; the tears were flooding out. Jas was trying to do most of the talking for me because I was unable to, but she said it was clear from the letter which was very articulate and explained my reasons very clearly. She could see from my reaction and my physical state that it was not good for me to prolong this pregnancy longer than necessary. She looked at the dates of our conception and said she believed I was not quite thirty-six and that she wouldn't take me to delivery until I was thirty-seven weeks. I told her I believed the dates she had were wrong as I knew exactly the date I ovulated and conceived. I told her I knew this as it was whilst I was on my Prince 2 course. Looking at these dates she agreed that we were so close to thirty-seven weeks that it would be okay for us to deliver the baby sooner. This was a huge relief to both of us.

There were a number of things that needed to be checked. One was that there was availability to deliver our child on the date of the 14 June. I would need to be in hospital for two days prior to that to have steroid injections to mature his lungs. We also discussed the fact that as I had opted to have a caesarean section, I would also need to see the anaesthetist. Whilst discussing it her assistant midwife went to see when I could see the anaesthetist. She came back with an appointment two days later which would have been the Friday of that week, exactly a week before my baby was due to be born. I thanked her so much for following our request and helping to put me at ease. We left the appointment extremely relieved knowing that our baby would be with us in nine days.

We started thinking about what we needed to do to prepare for that. One of the things was Jas explaining to his work that our baby was going to be delivered early so he would need to start his paternity leave. That was crucial as he was a team leader and they would need to put certain things in place for him to have his three weeks off. This was two week's paternity leave and one week's holiday. The other thing was Jas would not be able to attend the appointment with me on the Friday, so I asked my brother Steven to come with me as he was off work and had moved from London back to our family home. He was saving up for his own home. It was a blessing in disguise that he wasn't working at this time, he was able to help me with things that I needed and also Jas of course. So, I spoke to Steven and asked him to come Thursday night to attend this appointment with me on Friday and then stay over the weekend to help Jas put up the crib and Moses basket etc and assemble the car seat and everything else that we needed to have ready in time for me to go to hospital the following Wednesday. I asked him to keep these arrangements to himself.

At this point I was also being checked daily by the Wellbeing Centre at the hospital, so I was going from one appointment to the another. It was completely quite hectic but certainly reassuring as we were at this late stage now. The Wellbeing Centre knew how anxious I was, so they even arranged for me to have CTG scans over that last weekend whilst we were at home. My fingers had swelled up so much that I couldn't get my rings off. They were hurting, but there was nothing I could do about it and there was no way they were coming off unless they were cut them off and I certainly wasn't going down that route. I knew that the swelling would go down as soon as our little man was delivered.

Steven accompanied me to my two appointments on the Friday. The first one was with the Wellbeing Centre where he also learned that we were having a baby boy. The second was with the anaesthetist. The appointments had gone well and after Jas arrived home from work around 6:00 o'clock we decided to go out for dinner and just enjoy this time that we would have now before his long awaited arrival. We went to our local TGI's. We had a good laugh and a lovely meal. When we got back home; the little fellow was very active inside me. He put in his elbow and it was sticking out so far that you could see the shape of it on my stomach. It looked like something out of the Alien Movie. I got Steven to feel it and he was shocked at how sharp it was. He asked if it was hurting me and I told him it was uncomfortable but not really hurting. I explained that it hurts more when he kicks me in the ribs.

That weekend the weather was really warm and nice. We'd had some new garden furniture delivered around a week or two before in March when we'd had our garden redone, so that it was nice, landscaped and child friendly with slabs and some grass. It was low maintenance and just the type of garden we needed and wanted. I was very pleased with it because finally it was a garden that we could actually use. We had also had to change some of our fencing panels and Jas decided that weekend he would get rid of the mess because he knew he wasn't going to get a chance to do it again. Steven's girlfriend Grace joined us, and we sat outside eating our breakfast and enjoying the sun. Steven and Jas then cracked on with doing the work of setting up the crib sorting out the isofix in the car for the car seat and sorting out the bedding for the mattress cover on the Moses basket and the crib. I just sat back and relaxed, they took care of everything.

My hospital bag had been ready for several weeks following the growth scan in April, so everything was ready to go. I just needed to pack what I needed knowing that I was going to be in hospital now for five days, at least two days prior to the birth and two or three days after the birth as I was going to be having a C-section. I had already been told what I would need, so I had a bag that I would take with me and then an extra bag that would come at a later date. I didn't see the point in taking everything all in one go. There was no point in taking the babies bag straight away either because I knew I wasn't going to need that until the Friday. So, Jas would bring that on the morning of the C-section. Everything was in place and now we were just waiting for those last two days to go by.

Jas worked Monday and Tuesday in the office, and he completed everything that he needed to before saying that he was now off to be with me for the arrival of our baby boy. On the Wednesday I went into hospital. I had a private room and they monitored my blood levels and my sugar levels because I had gestational diabetes. They administered the steroids which was very uncomfortable I have to say, but it's what I needed to have done to bring my baby out into this world a bit earlier than it would normally be.

I took a couple of books with me, my iPod, phone charger and all those types of things. Jas paid for subscription on the hospital TV so that I could watch the programmes I enjoyed. That always started with Lorraine in the morning, then This Morning, followed by Loose Women and then ITV News. The afternoon would be spent reading or maybe watching a movie, but I was comfortable and relaxed and that was the main thing.

The ladies at the Wellbeing Centre also said that I could still go in for my appointments to have a scan and see little baby. I loved to do this as it gave me the added reassurance now that we were at that latter end. In some ways this was making me nervous and I was thinking, we are so close now, I hope nothing goes wrong. Jas would come and go during visiting hours although they weren't too strict with him because they knew how much we had gone through and that we were at that close up stage of delivery now. I had managed to get to know quite a few of the midwives quite well and they were very accommodating which was lovely. I had a visit from the manager of the midwives who I'd spoken to previously after making a complaint about the midwife that had not given me my scan before I was twenty-four weeks. She was so kind. She knew what we were going through and that we were having an early delivery. Everything was on standby just in case baby wasn't too well when he came out, so even the Neonatal Department was ready to take him in if needs be. It was really reassuring to have all this extra help on hand and when I was by myself it gave me time to reflect.

One of the biggest things I realised was that my prayers were being answered. I had written in my prayer at Coventry Cathedral that I wanted him to be born no later than a week before Luca's birthday, this was exactly what was happening now. Although I was nervous I still trusted God to deliver my baby perfectly healthy and safe.

On Thursday, my second day in the hospital and after having the steroid injections I became a little overindulgent at lunchtime, because they had one of my favourite desserts which is apple crumble and custard. I had a lighter lunch so that I had room for apple crumble thinking this would be okay. Well actually it wasn't okay. It spiked my blood sugar levels for my gestational diabetes. I had to then be monitored to see if it could be lowered and if not I would have to have an emergency C-section. I thought, how could I have been so stupid, sometimes my eyes are bigger than my belly and you just want what you want. But I should have known better. Sweet things are a big no-no for gestational diabetes. This panicked us a little bit and my mum and dad were visiting at this point as well. My mum although concerned was laughing a little only in the sense that she said you and your apple crumble, knowing me so well obviously. Jas on the other hand was quietly mad at me. He asked how I could be so stupid. I told him I knew now how stupid it had been, I just hadn't been thinking straight. Another part of me was thinking that I didn't want my baby to be born on the 13th as that would mean his first birthday next year would be on Friday the 13th and I was not having that for sure. I think everyone knows how I feel about Friday the 13th now, considering that was the date of Luca's growth scan. I've hated the date ever since.

My mum told us not to focus on this and to just hope that the baby was okay. The midwife was very understanding and said she couldn't resist apple crumble either. She smiled at me whilst everyone else was angry at me. She suggested they just gave me lots of water to see if that would bring my sugar levels down. I drank lots of jugs of cold water keep and they checked every hour to see if my levels were coming down.

When my mum and dad left Jas was still moaning at me for being so thoughtless. I told him that he was just going to keep moaning he might as well go home and that I'd be quite happy by myself drinking water and watching telly. I even said that 'The Good Wife' was going to come on soon and that as it's one of my favourite programmes, I'd like to watch it in peace and quiet without you moaning at me and I huffed and puffed. He did end up going home and I was relieved because he was doing my head in. My sugar levels were already starting to come down, so I told him there was nothing to worry about I'd see him in the morning as planned for the delivery of our baby. I also reminded him not to forget the bag with the things we needed for the baby.

Actually, Steven was going to be dropping Jas off at the hospital the following day because of the parking charges. We knew we were going to be there all day and it was just silly to pay such charges, so this is what had been happened for the previous days too. The next day, it would be much earlier, but Steven was fine with that.

So, Jas went home, and I sat back on the bed drinking water and watching 'The Good Wife.' My sugar levels had come right down so everything was safe again. After 'The Good Wife' finished at 10 o'clock I decided I better get some sleep in, so I put some calming music on my iPod, stuck in my earphones and hoped to drift off nicely. My head was spinning with all sorts though. I wondered about whether everything was going to go okay, whether my baby would be well, whether he would need to go into neonatal care and that if he did, how I would feel guilty. All these things were just going round and around in my head. We had pushed for this early delivery and as much as I needed this for my own sanity, I was praying that I wasn't putting my baby in any danger. What if something happened in these last stages and he didn't make it. What if within these last few hours whatever happened with Luca that made his heart stop, what if it happens again and I'm so close to having him in my arms.

After losing Luca, I had become the type of person that thought the worst was always going to happen. I'd never been like this prior to that, but from then, I always thought about what if this happens, or what if that happens. I couldn't ever stop focusing on the negatives. It had become a way of thinking not just in relation to my baby but for everything. Even if Jas was just a little late coming home from work I would wonder if he was okay and if he'd been in a car accident I'd call him, but obviously didn't want him to answer if he was driving, which he didn't, as he didn't have a car kit in at the time, so I would just wait and wait and wait and think and think and think. I had become one of those negative people now, when before in life I'd always been quite positive and looked at the things with a cup half full mentality not a cup half empty, but after losing Luca nothing made sense anymore, statistics meant nothing to me. For example, there is around a one percent chance that someone will have a stillborn however it had happened to me, so now when anybody ever says quotes this statistic I just look at them. It happened to me and there was no cause for it. He was perfectly fine as so people can shove their statistics where the sun doesn't shine. That's how I felt when anybody threw any sort of statistics at me. That night, I drifted in and out of sleep, but I never really got a proper sleep.

The next morning, I woke up early. I had a shower and put on the gown that I was given, ready to be called to go down. Whilst in the shower Jas arrived. The first thing I checked was that he had the bag. I opened it up, took out the clothes that I needed and the nappy. I was excited and nervous all at the same time. We sat and waited and waited, as the anaesthetist was running late. There had been an emergency C-section that he'd had to attend to, so understandably we had to wait a bit longer. Jas took a photo of me sitting in my chair holding my bump for the last time. Then I took a photo of him, half laying down on my bed, just smiling. He was protesting at having his photo taken as he always does. We didn't actually talk about much; we just had the news on catching up with current affairs but neither of us were actually really listening to this. I think we were both just alone with our thoughts about the impending arrival of our little boy.

Finally, the anaesthetist arrived, and we were ushered downstairs to the Delivery Theatre. At this point Jas and I were separated as they needed to get me ready and wired up to the machines. It was hard for them to find a vein where they could administer the canula and then they struggled to keep me still long enough to administer the spinal injection to numb me. I don't know exactly how long this all took but once I was numb and laying on the bed, Jas came through the door covered in surgical gowns and took a seat next to me. He held my hand and he had the camera. We just looked at each other mentally saying to each other well here we go, this is it now. This is the time. We were smiling at each other as we were finally at the point that we had been waiting for all these nine months. By now, those months felt like 12 years.

They didn't tell me anything that they were doing, like cutting me or anything like that. I was quite glad actually because I didn't want to know anything. I think I had already told them not to tell me and to just get on with it. Soon enough I could feel the pulling and plodding around in my stomach. It didn't hurt, I could just feel the movements. I was waiting calmly but I was a little anxious. Then we finally heard the little cry and we beamed from ear to ear and shed a little tear that finally he was here, he was out, and he was crying.

He was brought round by the midwife crying gently and obviously cold. She gave him a quick check over. We could see her doing it from where we were. We just looked on, full of emotion once he cried and kicked around his arms and legs as if to say I'm cold. Then she bought him over to me for skin contact and as soon as he heard my voice and he was on my skin he stopped crying. He put his little fingers in my mouth, I said:

"Hiya my handsome boy."

Wow what a feeling that was. It was the best feeling in the world. He fell asleep on me immediately and seemed very comfortable on his mummy. This just added to the amazement I was feeling at the time. The midwife took a few pictures of him on me which I cherish and look at quite often even now. The skin to skin contact felt like just a minute but it was probably more like 5 minutes, but it certainly wasn't long enough for me.

The midwife picked him up again and told him she needed to do some further checks and then she'd get him dressed and bring him back to us. Whilst the checks were being done, Jas took some photos. He was kicking his legs and arms about as if still trying to say he was cold and in my mind, probably also saying that he wanted his mummy back.

After what felt like quite a while, we were told by our surgeon that the cord had been wrapped around our little baby's neck twice, so it had taken them longer to get him out because they had to be very careful. I gasped in shock but was so thankful that he was okay. The doctor continued to tell us that my placenta had not detached very well and so they had to cut it out which is why it took longer for them to stitch me up. This was the same thing that had happened when Luca was born. Again, they said it was quite normal and I told them it had happened with our first child too. Whilst still waiting for them to sort out our new baby boy whom we had already decided to name Ky, I thought to myself gosh if I had not insisted on Ky being born early, he may not have been here at all, with the cord being wrapped around his neck twice. If I had gone full term, that would have tightened and ultimately ended his life too. I was so thankful and grateful to God. I closed my eyes and thanked God that he was here safe and that the prayer that I had written at Coventry Cathedral had been answered word by word.

Soon we were ready to be moved to the recovery area. The doctors told me everything had been stitched up well and I hadn't lost a lot of blood and I was okay. The midwife assured me that all of Ky's checks had also been fine. In the recovery area Ky was in his little cot and I was offered a mug of tea and jam on toast which I really needed by this time. Jas was taking photos whilst I was eating. We could not stop smiling, while looking at our gorgeous little boy. He resembled Luca quite a lot, this was another thing that I had actually put in my prayer at the cathedral as I had said I wanted him to resemble his brother but I didn't want him to be spitting image of him. That part of my prayer was also answered and had come true. God had listened to all my prayers and I was extremely grateful and thankful.

After I had finished eating the midwife came in and asked if I would like to feed my little baby. I was excited for this part. I had already decided that I wanted to breastfeed, so she picked him up and brought him over to me and he latched on straight away. I exclaimed out loud about what an amazing and awesome feeling it was. He was going for it; he was obviously very hungry. The midwife smiled and told me I was doing a great job. I just smiled at him as he suckled away to get his milk.

She kept coming back to check his temperature. He wasn't regulating his temperature as he should have been by this point and she was a little concerned. I asked if there was something wrong and she said no, but that he should be getting warmer than he is. She decided to take him to the lamp room and put him under a warming lamp to bring his temperature up. I had never heard of a warming lamp for babies and grew a little concerned.

"Is he going to be okay?" I asked nervously.

She knew our history and assured us that he was perfectly fine and just needed a little bit more warming up and that it wasn't uncommon. She wheeled him off to this other room which was along the corridor to one side and in there she took off Ky's clothes and lay him under this lamp. He was clearly very comfortable with this being done she suggested to Jas that he went to make some phone calls as we'd be here for a good fifteen minutes.

So, Jas went outside to make his calls first to Steven and then our parents and then his sister. He knew my mum would call my family, and that Steven obviously already knew, and that Sunny my other brother was working abroad again so we couldn't contact him. Everyone was so delighted. They hadn't expected him to be arriving so soon. We hadn't told anybody apart from Steven, so it came as a brilliant surprise. Everyone thought I was in hospital for a couple of days to have the steroids but then go home, they didn't know he was going to be this early. Before Jas even got back to the room, he was receiving messages of congratulations from friends and family. News spread very quickly once it is out.

Ky had been warming up nicely and his temperature had risen so the midwife thought he'd be fine now and told us we'd get his clothes on and then she'd take us back up to our room on the Maternity Ward. I was feeling extremely exhausted. I think this was due to the sheer relief of his safe arrival and the lack of sleep I'd had the night before, along with what had felt like twelve years of anxiety throughout the pregnancy. In addition, the drugs that I had been given for the caesarean section were also making me feel drowsy, so by this point I wanted nothing but to sleep. Ky was content and asleep so it was a good time for us both to get some rest.

Jas decided to go home and have something to eat and agreed that Steven would come and sit with me and the midwife staff were fine with this. Steven would park outside, and Jas would jump in, and then Steven could come up to my room. When Steven saw Ky he remarked on how absolutely gorgeous he was. I knew I was biased but agreed he was totally right. I had told Steven beforehand that when he came to the hospital to see Ky he should bring my Arsenal scarf as I wanted to take some photos of Ky with the scarf before Jas got back to the hospital. Before Jas had left when I was sleeping however, he had taken his own photos of Ky with his Everton scarf. Clearly, we both had the same idea but hadn't told each other.

We already knew who he would support. In the March before, when Everton were still in the FA Cup and Arsenal were already out of it, and Everton were also a few points ahead of us in the table, Jas and I made a bet. Jas had proposed that if Everton won The FA Cup, Ky was going to be an Everton supporter and the backup was that whichever team finished higher up in the League that's who he would support. At this point Jas was so convinced that Everton were going to win the FA Cup and that they would finish higher in the League than Arsenal, but being a true Gooner Girl, I knew that Arsenal would come back and I would win this bet . In true Arsenal style we did exactly that, so I had won the bet and now Ky was going to be an Arsenal supporter, well at least until he could decide for himself as he grew older. Steven draped the Arsenal scarf around Ky. He was fast asleep in his cot and we took some photos. He then held Ky and had a few photos taken with the Arsenal scarf there still. He put Ky back into his cot and I told him we'd both go to sleep for a while. Luckily there was a paper left lying around, so Steven read this whilst we slept.

I think we slept for about an hour and then it was feeding time again. The midwife came in and asked if I was ready to feed the little man again and I replied that I was. She picked him up brought him over to me but this time he was not latching on. She said this could happen sometimes and that maybe he just needed a little bit more skin to skin contact. I didn't want him to go cold again as he'd been put under the heat lamp earlier, so she suggested that we didn't take all of his clothes off, just the top layer, and so that is what we did. He did then latch on and took some milk.

I had missed out on lunch so the midwife said she would get me some sandwiches and asked if I would like a cup of tea. I love my tea so I told her yes, a cup of tea would be amazing. She came back shortly after with a sandwich and a cup of tea. Ky seemed to have finished feeding so after I winded him and she lay him down. Whilst eating and drinking I was chatting with Steven and telling him how amazing it was when we heard his cry, and also about the fact that the cord had been wrapped around his neck twice.

Steven was shocked and thought the same way it was so good that we'd pushed for him to be born early. God knows what would have happened otherwise.

During this time, many midwives came in to see Ky, those from the Wellbeing Centre and also the Head Obstetrician who had given us the go-ahead to have him delivered early. I was told later that actually she doesn't make many visits, so we were very privileged. I thought it was nice, she clearly wanted to make sure we were both okay, as we had taken the risk of having him a little earlier than we were supposed to. They were all delighted to see him here safe and well.

It was quite late afternoon by this stage. Jas had called Steven to say that he'd had a shower, a rest, something to eat and was now ready to swap. He told Steven he 'd set off and would be there shortly. So, Steven gave me a big hug and Ky a kiss on his forehead and said he'd see us tomorrow because other visitors would want to come and see us later and he'd had some quality time with us both already. I agreed that was a thoughtful idea, thanked him for coming, told him I loved him lots and thanked him for everything he'd been doing for us. Steven replied that it had been his pleasure and he loved me lots too.

Soon after Jas arrived and asked how his little baby boy was and I told him he was fine, and he'd had some more milk. I also explained that I'd had something to eat and a cup of tea and we'd both had a sleep as well. Jas was going to be staying overnight. He was going to be sleeping in the chair next to me. This had already been arranged prior to the birth with the Head of the Midwives. He had freshened up and brought the clothes that he needed for the evening and the next day. We knew that the next day he would be able to go home and freshen up again properly and change his clothes unlike myself of course.

I needed to keep my water intake up and a jug of cold water had been left, so that I could drink it as and when I needed it. My sugar levels were still being monitored as I'd had gestational diabetes. To my surprise they had already started lowering. I hadn't thought that would happen so soon after the delivery, but it was pretty much immediate. I was craving some chocolate. I had asked Jas to bring some just in case I could eat some. The next time she took my blood sugars I asked the midwife if as it was all normal again could I have some sugar in my tea and she said I could. So, I enquired as to whether that meant I could also have some chocolate and she laughed and explained that I could, as long as it wasn't too much and that she'd be keeping an eye on my levels. Finally, I was going to have some chocolate this was great as it had been the hardest thing not to eat during this pregnancy with me being such a chocoholic. My favourite is Cadburys chocolate and that's what Jas had bought for me, so it was nice to have a couple of pieces of Dairy Milk, not many pieces of course, but it did the job that's for sure.

Before we knew it, visiting time was close by. We had already made it clear to our parents and siblings that only they were allowed to come, no uncles, no aunties, no cousins, nobody else only our parents and siblings. We knew we were going to be there another night anyway so we said the others could come the day after. The first to arrive was Jas's mum and dad along with his sister. They were just beaming with pride immediately when they saw Ky. Immediately Jas's sister said that he looked just like me and was fair-skinned too. They had probably been there about ten minutes before my parents arrived. They were all in the room at the same time which was not usually allowed so I assumed the staff hadn't realised. Everyone was talking about how beautiful he was, how blessed we were to have a baby boy and how much he resembled Luca too. It was lovely just having a few people there talking. Jas's sister was the first to leave and then it was just the grandparents left. They didn't want to leave too soon but also they didn't want to stay too long, because they could see that I was exhausted. My dad took some pictures. He'd brought his own camera and mum took some on her phone because there were quite a few people that were saying send us a photo as soon as you can. I had already sent photos to some people during the day. My phone was on silent, but I had been receiving a lot of messages. Steven had asked me if I wanted him to announce the good news on Facebook. I agreed he could do this and tag me in so that all my friends could see it too. I'd had a quick look at Facebook, and we had received a huge amount of congratulations.

It was just before 7:30 p.m. before our parents left and then we got settled for the evening. I had already had dinner before they had arrived and as Jas was staying over, he was also allowed to have some, but he hadn't wanted much as he had eaten at home. After they all left, it was time to feed Ky again before we could settle in and fall asleep. After his feed and putting him on his back to wind him he settled back into his cot and went fast asleep. Jas made himself comfortable on the chair and I was on the bed. I was still unable to go to the bathroom. I was still numb from the waist down. I had a catheter which had been emptied and then reattached. Everything was fine so we could just drift off to sleep. That was easier said than done however, as although I was exhausted, we were right next to the doors that would constantly open to take women down to the Labour Ward. I didn't want to put in my earplugs just in case I didn't hear Ky. So, it was very much a hit and miss sleep. Ky was really good in the night. He slept really well. I thought this was a good start and I hope it continues. I had to wake him up a couple of times for feeding but he settled back down very quickly. I was getting a good couple of hours at a time. I would wake up after hearing some noise and then have to try to go back to sleep. It was like that all night long really.

The next morning, I woke up feeling more refreshed than I thought I would. Ky had been great all night. Jas said that he barely heard him. I told him I knew; I could hear him snoring through it and we looked at each other and laughed. I told him that he seemed to have had a better sleep than I did as the doors that were opening constantly and it kept waking me up. He said he didn't notice them very much and I said that was because he's a heavy sleeper. Little Ky did not hear them either. I was the only one that was really bothered.

The breakfast trolley was outside so Jas went to get some cereal and tea for me, and some cereal for himself also. The midwife came in after breakfast to check my sugar levels which had come down back to normal. She told us she'd do it once more later and then if it was still normal, then they wouldn't need to do it again.

Then it was time to feed Ky again. This time he didn't seem to be latching on properly and was fidgety, letting out a little cry as though he was still hungry. The midwife wondered if my milk flow was not coming through properly, so she did some manual checking. She was right it wasn't coming through enough, so to fill him up so we decided to manually pump some off to give to Ky with a syringe and then we would have to top him up with formula. This seemed to work and helped him to be content which is what we needed. She told us they'd keep a check on this whilst we were in the hospital so they could see exactly how much milk was actually coming through. She explained that sometimes it just takes a while for it to start coming through fully, but at least we can try these other things whilst you're at the hospital. This was a relief for me knowing that he would be getting the good stuff from me and being topped up with formula, so it wasn't just giving up and going straight to formula.

Steven and Jas had swapped through the day again and as Steven had some time with Ky again, he said that he would not then come in the evening. That evening however it got really busy with our parents, siblings, cousins, uncles, aunts, and my grandmother who was the only remaining great grandparent all coming to see our little man. I think we must have had about thirty visitors in there at one point. The midwife came in saying that she knew this was a very joyous time for all our family considering what we'd been through before, but there was just too many here and they must start going. I asked my uncle to relay the message to everyone that was in the waiting area which was actually not an official waiting area either. That two-hour visiting time was exhausting and Ky was a little fidgety.

Once everybody went I fed him and hoped he would settle, but he had quite an unsettled night unfortunately. It was definitely not like the night before. Jas and I were up with him so much and then when he did finally sleep so did Jas however, I wasn't as fortunate and didn't fall asleep like they did. Jas was snoring and Ky was up every other hour, so I was getting an hour at a time, but the midwives on night shift were fantastic and really did help me.

The next morning, I was exhausted. I felt like I had no energy to even pick Ky up. We had to have a few checks done to see if there was any chance of him going home. These included checking his weight, seeing if he was feeding okay, checking on how I was doing after having a caesarean section. I was desperate to go home. I knew that if we stayed in the hospital any longer I would not sleep properly and that Ky would be more unsettled. I really wanted to get into a routine at home, in our own place, in our comfort zone. The first appointment was to go and see the midwife down the corridor. Both Jas and I took Ky to have his weight checked and other things that they needed to do. They wrote these in his red book. As we were from an ethnic background, they also asked if there was any chance that anybody had been abroad who had come to see him as even weeks after they returned they could pass on something. We did not want him to pick up any bugs, so we agreed that we wanted him to be given an appropriate injection to protect him.

Next we had breakfast. I actually felt so exhausted that I couldn't even feed myself. I had half of what was there, had my cup of tea and then lay back and said I just needed to sleep for a while as it had been an exhausting night. Ky was settled so I tried to get some sleep in, and Jas started packing the bags in the hope that we could go home. Whilst I was sleeping a midwife came and said Ky could have his jab and we should bring him down the corridor again. I was so exhausted I literally could not lift my head. I cried. Jas asked why I was crying, and I told him that I felt like a useless mother. Already I was so exhausted that I couldn't even pick my own baby up and walk him down for his jab. Jas just hugged me and told me not to worry and to rest and he'd take him for his jab. He said they wouldn't be long, and I was not a useless mother, just really tired. He knew it hadn't been an easy night for me and that things would be easier once we got home.

After I'd had some sleep we were all back in the room together. I suggested that we finished packing the bags and said I was going to insist that we went home today because it was not good for me to stay here and I'd already been there since Wednesday. I had no desire to stay any longer. Jas had done most of the packing already, so I just needed to make sure that everything else was done. It barely took anytime at all. As I still wasn't really getting around easily, I told Jas what to do.

He then got the camcorder out and we filmed Ky and were saying hopefully will be going home soon. It's so much fun to watch those films back now and hear the little cry that he used to give out. At this point he also had a lot of phlegm in his mouth and on his chest and we put him gently on his back to get this phlegm out. It's all on camera but it's good stuff to show him as he's getting older. It was almost lunchtime before we got the go ahead that we could go home. We called Steven to bring the car. He parked close to the front because we had so many things to put in the car. Jas carried Ky down the stairs and I walked very slowly behind them.

When we arrived home my neighbours were looking out their windows and they waved through the windows and shouted their congratulations. We gave them a little peek of Ky in his car seat and then went inside, where we were greeted by Jas's mum and dad. They had bought some food over and just wanted to be there for when Ky arrived home. They didn't stay too long, and we really needed to catch up on our sleep and settle Ky at home . This is exactly what we did, and it was so nice. I was really grateful just to be back at my own home.

That night was so lovely. I felt like I was living a dream. Ky was at home with us and we couldn't stop taking photos of him in our bedroom, just the three of us together. We hadn't actually set up our baby sensor for the cot so all night I would wake up to check on his every little movement and sound. I was almost jumping up as much as I could with the stitches. Needless to say, the following day I got Jas to set it up. The monitor would put my mind at ease because it would monitor Ky's heartbeat and breathing throughout the night without me having to keep jumping up to check on him. So, it was a must in my book.

Summary

When you go on to have another pregnancy after losing a baby it is full of anxiety. All of the innocent enjoyment of what you should feel during a pregnancy is taken away and a pregnancy that is nine months feels like nine plus years. I think for me and many others it would have felt like this whether I had left it two years before trying again or not. I think at any stage that you decide to have a rainbow child, it will always be filled with that fear of loss again.

Although people want to say congratulations when they hear that you are pregnant again, it's extremely bittersweet. You almost want to say keep your congratulations until the baby is here safely, but again with the way society is, we can't actually say the things that we really want to. Even though we have been through hell, we are still the ones that have to bite our tongue, so we don't offend anybody else.

What other people need to learn from this is that when an Angel Warrior goes on to have another pregnancy, please do not say everything will be okay this time, because in their mind nothing is okay until the baby is actually healthy and in their arms. Do not say you will have your baby back now. This baby is not a replacement for the baby they have lost, and it is not the same baby coming back, this is a different baby.

As an Angel Warrior you are more than entitled to ask for extra checks and seek reassurance. You need to help you through this pregnancy, and no one should be denying you this. This is where I feel the NHS needs to adapt more. If a parent that they are taking care of now has gone though the most horrific thing of losing a child previously, they should be given extra support and care for their next pregnancy. I was clearly ignored and dealt with very rudely by the midwife who refused to let me have checks on Ky before I was twenty-four weeks. I feel a minority of midwives lack empathy for those that have lost a baby and are full of anxiety in their subsequent pregnancy. If I had not complained about her to the Head of the Midwives at the hospital, I probably wouldn't have got the extra special treatment that I did thereafter. Sometimes it is upon us sadly, to insist that we are taken better care of, so that our babies can be bought into the world alive, healthy, and safe.

Chapter Four
New Normal

It was so lovely having Ky at home and finally having a healthy baby in my arms. I was really enjoying being a mother, bathing my baby, looking after him and doing all those enjoyable things that I should have had right at the beginning with Luca. The following week was the first anniversary of Luca's death and also what would have been his first birthday. I always keep them separate because the eighteenth is when he grew his Angel wings and died in my womb and the twenty-first is when I gave birth to him and saw his beautiful face for the first time. The twenty-first will always remain his birthday and the eighteenth will always remain the anniversary of his death.

Some people that we weren't very close to had asked if they could come over and see Ky. They had insensitively asked if they could come on the twenty-first and I'd told them no it wasn't a good day for us. I got a reply saying, "sorry I forgot." Clearly people had already forgotten about Luca. She went on to say, "that at least you have another baby now, and that will help you move on." I thought no one moves on from the death of a child, another child does not replace the child you have lost. I just wanted to scream at the people that were making these comments. What were they thinking, it's one thing not being able to know what to say, but it's another to be saying the most stupid, insensitive, ridiculous things!

That week was extremely bittersweet. Only two days before Luca's anniversary we were home with Ky, and my prayers had been answered. Ky was in my arms before Luca's anniversary and his birthday. I'm so glad he was here for us, because this week was hard enough to go through and would have been even harder if he had not been in my arms.

Luca's first birthday was extremely emotional, my first child my first son was having his first birthday in heaven, not here, where we would have been throwing a big party for him. I could not hug him, kiss him, hold him, shower him with my love and gifts. Instead I bought a small cake, put a number one candle on it and his photo next to it and we blew out the candle together. Afterwards, Ky was in Jas's arms and I sobbing on the sofa.

Jas was off work for three weeks we had built a routine that we could continue when Jas went back to work. It was lovely having that time together, something we had waited to have for so long. We were sharing duties, which made me a little worried about how I would cope once he was back at work, as I'd be doing it all. Back then we didn't have a dishwasher. We did go on to get one when Ky was six months old, after I won the poker match at our family Christmas games. I put my winnings towards getting that. The washing of all the bottles was so much easier after that and I kicked myself for not getting one before. Hindsight is a beautiful thing.

The midwife came and checked on Ky and thankfully he was putting on the weight that he had lost and was thriving. This was extremely reassuring for us as it is for any parent. We didn't allow lots of people to come and see Ky. We actually decided that the ones that would be able to come and see him were the ones that had supported us and came to see us when Luca had died.

We also decided that as there were so many people that were asking to see Ky that we would have what Indians called a Kheer Party. This is a party to celebrate the birth of a child. We decided we would have this after his first lot of jabs. So, it would be just after he was eight weeks old. We hired a Community Hall, booked caterers and there would be 120 people attending. We planned everything for the party whilst Jas was still off work.

A week before the party we had gone to a photographer to have some beautiful photos of the three of us taken and lots of Ky in some very cute poses such as being in a basket, with blankets and beautiful hats on him. Some of these were while he was awake and a lot when he was asleep. I cherish those photos. They are my absolute favourite ones that were taken when he was a baby.

Ky was wonderful throughout the party. He stayed asleep for most of it and only actually woke up for a feed and a nappy change. Whilst he was asleep, he was in his pushchair as I didn't want everybody holding him and it was a good excuse to stop germs being spread around him.

We had music playing, and the drinks were flowing. Everybody was in a mighty good mood celebrating the birth of Ky.

During the party there was a little bit of dancing. I'd had this lovely balloon arch made with Ky's name on it. The male of the couple that had always been so nasty during the early months of losing Luca, took down the named balloons and broke them and stamped on them as if in rage expressing he was not being happy for us. My family were utterly shocked and asked what on earth he was doing. I couldn't understand why he would be doing this, I only realised months later that it was because they weren't actually pleased that we'd had a healthy son. Jas was so out of it with having had celebratory shots with everybody and doing cheers to the birth of his son, that he didn't notice any of this happening. When we got home, I had to get Jas to bed which was quite funny, whilst Ky was laying in his cot awake and kicking away making up for all the sleep that he'd had during the day.

The next day, Jas was hungover and as Ky had gone to sleep later than he would normally he was out of sots a little. I told Jas all about the things at the party that he couldn't remember.

Ky's first Christmas was amazing. He was dressed as a little Santa and he was spoilt with love and gifts by the whole family. We were all together at my parent's home, the family home where we all grew up. Time was flying now that we had our handsome little Ky in our lives.

As I had been made redundant just before Ky was due to be born I was able to have eighteen months off with Ky which was fantastic and a proper start to motherhood with my little baby. I loved seeing all the changes, his first words and there were lots of milestones that I was at home for.

During this time, the legal case we had started for Luca's medical negligence continued. One independent midwife had stated she believed there was negligence involved, but the independent obstetrician thought that there hadn't been and said there was no guarantee that Luca would have survived. As he had the final say, the case came to a close with no justice for Luca. I was fuming, I wanted a third person to make a decision. This was completely unfair and unfounded in our eyes. The solicitor said we could carry on with the case but would need to pay. Sadly, we didn't have the money to carry on with it. Surely it made sense to get another verdict if one says yes and the other says no, but apparently that is not how it works. Even with the facts that they had about Ky's growth scan which was almost identical to Luca's and the fact that I was put on weekly and eventually daily scanning with Ky didn't matter. Surely if they had done that with Luca, they would have noticed he had stopped growing at some point and that they needed to get him out after which I believe he would have survived. To us, it was complete and utter negligence that had lost us our son and there was now nothing we could do about it. We were heartbroken that there was no justice for Luca, and even more so that this midwife who had missed the warning signs on his growth scan could be doing this to more families. I wanted to stop her, but now I was helpless to do so.

Eventually as my statutory maternity pay stopped, we were struggling financially. I knew that I did want to go back to work and that nursery would be good for Ky as he would learn so much. He was so clingy to me and it would be a great way for him to start socialising with others. I started looking for work after his first birthday which had been lovely. We did a little party for him in the Community Hall in our village with just the closest family children and our friends' children who he was growing up with. We just kept it to young children under seven. So, it didn't cost very much, a children's party only with nothing really for the adults in contrast to what we'd done when he was born. We just bought a few beers and a bit of food for the adults that were attending with their children. It was mainly a children's party which was lovely.

We had to invite the couple that had caused so much trouble by this point. They arrived late and left early thankfully and also did not talk to us nor acknowledge the birthday boy. Soon after the party we cut ties with them completely and have ever since. They had caused a lot of arguments in our marriage months earlier when Ky was about eight months old. Jas and I had a huge argument based on some comments that they had made, and Jas couldn't understand why I was still taking it so personally about Luca. Finally I burst out the words that I had been holding on to for so long, I asked him, how would you feel if Luca had died in your arms, because he died in my body and that will stay with me forever!!

In that moment Jas finally got it and we both held each other and cried. Ky was in his cot awake but kicking away oblivious to what was happening between his parents, luckily. All of this had put me into a depression, and I had sought help from my GP. I was put on antidepressants in February 2014. I was still grieving for Luka and still wanted to be the best mum I could be for Ky, but it was all very overwhelming, and had started to affect our marriage.

A few weeks after taking the antidepressants things started to get better. When my GP asked how things were going, I told him that I knew it might sound strange but I am starting to love my husband again, we both laughed and he told me that was a really good sign so I knew I was on the right track by taking the pills. We had cut all ties with the insensitive couple and were now in a much better place in our marriage.

My mom knew that we were struggling financially and that I was looking for a job, but she desperately wanted me to stay at home as long as I could with Ky. So, my parents gave us £5,000 so that I could be off a little longer and not have to stress about money. I had enrolled Ky into our local nursery and went with him at first to get him settled into the new environment. I was applying for jobs but obviously didn't know when one would come up, so it was the sensible thing to start getting him settled at the nursery where he would be full time once I took up a new role.

In the November 2014, I was due to be at an interview for large corporate company. A few days before the interview I came down with laryngitis and had to email the agency to let them know I could not attend. They questioned whether I was serious about attending the interview and I told them I absolutely was but couldn't be at an interview if I couldn't talk. Luckily, it was rearranged for about ten days later. I had two interviews all on the same day, one with the person who would be my line manager and the other with who would be my department manager. The interviews went very well and the following afternoon I found out that I had got the job. They wanted me to start a week before Christmas just to get the nitty gritty out of the way, so that I could start my full role in the new year. I said I would have to check when the nursery could take Ky full time as that was the biggest part of the equation. In addition, as the nursery closes over Christmas I would not be able to work all the days over Christmas, as Jas was also working some of the days too. We came to some compromises and the nursery luckily said that they could take him the week before Christmas as many children would already be going home and starting their Christmas holidays with their parents, so that was extremely fortunate timing for us.

In the couple of weeks leading up to me starting my full time job, I was taking Ky into nursery for full days a couple of times a week so he would get used to it. When I started my job, it felt quite daunting as I hadn't worked since Luca had died. But I soon got my feet under the table and settled into the job pretty quickly. Everybody was so nice which made it even better.

Now that we were going to have two incomes coming in we splashed out a little bit over Christmas and bought some things that we would never have been able to get before. We just did that little bit extra for each other. Normally it was Jas and I that always went without but this time we could actually buy presents for each other too. Jas had been wanting a Samsung tablet for quite a while but we could never have afforded it before so that is what I got from his boys for Christmas. We have always made a point of making sure Luca is part of our Christmases and any occasions in between, such as birthdays Mother's Days, and Father's Days. Sometimes we would get a present from each of our boys but sometimes it's been something big from both of them together. No matter what, we have always made sure he's included and that's what we'll always continue to do for the rest of our lives too.

This was now Ky's second Christmas and he was into everything. He was obviously more concerned about ripping the paper off the presents than the presents themselves. We got lots of toys and some clothes which he just threw across the room as any child would at eighteen months. He was so funny at this age, he quite liked taking selfies and was finding his feet now, walking around holding furniture. He was just on the edge of being able to walk unaided but not quite there. It was a quiet Christmas. Normally we would all get together at my mum and dad's house in Leicestershire but this time they came to us with my brother Steven. It was ever so cute because Ky was playing with his toys and all the focus was on him because he was a funny little character by that point. The year before, his first Christmas he'd been dressed up as a little Santa and was just six months old. He loved laughing at silly things and noises, which was so cute, and everybody just wanted to be holding him and cuddling him as he was a chubby little fella. This year he was dressed up as a little elf. He was so cute again and would look down at his clothes and pull at the tassels which were on the legs of the elf suit. It was a wonderful cosy Christmas at home which was just what we needed. We had bought him a toy which was a little dog that you put batteries in and it would bark and walk along. I thought he would love it because he liked dogs, but he hated it and was quite scared by it. It and took him a while to get to like it but he still loves it to this day now.

The next day was a nice lazy Boxing Day which we always had every year, but this one I've never forgotten as its when Ky started walking by himself. I was giddy with excitement that he could walk from room to room without either of us, it was lovely. I watch the video clips of it to this day, watching him walking along whilst he was eating his Wotsits.

We were now at a point at which we were living our lives again. It was not that we had got over the loss of Luca as I've said, no parent ever gets over the loss of her child, but we were finding our feet again and had started to enjoy life since Ky had been born. Slowly but surely we got to the point where we were far better, the antidepressants had played a part in this and we were getting our focus back. Once I had started work I began to feel like a bit of the old me again but I would never fully be that person again because when you lose a child part of you dies with your child, but I was in a good place and that was a great feeling. I knew now that I didn't need the antidepressants, so I saw my GP and said that I wanted to come off them. This has to be a slow process because you cannot suddenly come off antidepressants you have to wean yourself off them.

We also decided we wanted to take a holiday. This would be our first holiday since going to Rome after Luca died. Now it was actually going to be a family holiday, just the three of us. So, it had to be a lovely place with a beach, child and family friendly. We found the perfect place. After I got my first pay cheque in January we booked our holiday. We arranged to go to Gran Canaria, a place in the South part, called Puerto Rico. We stayed by the marina and it was just a couple of minutes' walk to the beach and there were restaurants surrounding the apartment suites that we were staying in. It was wonderful. Ky was great on the flight and slept most of the way there and on the way back. The actual holiday was fantastic too. We thoroughly enjoyed it and we've been back there every year since. The locals know us now and they've seen Ky grow up.

It was now March 2015 and when we did come back from our holiday as we'd they really loved it, we decided to book another holiday for Ky's second birthday which was going to be in the June. Every June now Jas and I take our fortnight's holiday so that we are off for Ky's birthday and also Luca's birthday the week after. On Luca's birthday, we always go to the place where we scattered his ashes in a way to visit him. We always cut a cake for him and I kiss a balloon and send it off into the sky for him to catch. I also always posted something on Facebook on Mother's Day, referring to my two gorgeous boys. Luca is always included in everything for us.

The first few months when Ky started nursery he was constantly catching bugs, colds, tonsillitis, and everything. We had been warned that when a child does start nursery they will pick up everything that's going. So, often there were times when we'd get home and I have to take it in turns looking after our sick child because now we were both full time working parents. By the end of March going into early April all this began to stop and it was great to have that respite. We had now booked our holiday to Portugal for Ky's second birthday.

That year we also had my brother Steven's wedding. He was marrying his girlfriend Grace and I was so looking forward to their wedding. The wedding was set for August. Jas and I had decided we were going to try for another baby, but I said let's put off trying until after Steven's wedding as I wanted to be able to enjoy it without being in the early stages of pregnancy. So, we agreed that I would come off the contraceptive pill in preparation and that's exactly what we were going to do.

Time was flying by and the Portugal holiday had come and gone so quick. It was beautiful, and we had a great holiday, but it wasn't as nice as Gran Canaria. We made the most of it, nonetheless. I think when you find somewhere that you love so much, it's hard to beat it and when you have set the bar high, you now compare everything to that one place that was just magical.

As we were still off for another week, we did a few day trips with Ky and obviously went to Luca's resting place. It is so peaceful and beautiful along the river and it's in a very quiet village of Leicestershire.

Work was great and I was fully settled in. We had so many projects that were going on, but it was really enjoyable too and nice and flexible. I had one day of working at home and four days in the office. Jas also did this, on the days we worked from home, we were able to collect Ky earlier from nursery, which was really nice.

Suddenly Steven's wedding was upon us and we were all so excited. Ky looked so cute in his waistcoat and cravat. Grace looked stunning and Steven was so handsome in his tuxedo. I was so proud of both of them, my little brother the baby of the family who was getting married. At other parties, weddings, and everything like that, before Luca had died, I'd be on the dance floor non-stop but some part of that had died in me. Although I danced and thoroughly enjoyed the wedding, I wasn't constantly on the dance floor, so this was different for me. There were times where I would just go off and look after the children who were all playing together, then I'd come back when some of my favourite songs were playing. These were mostly R&B and hip hop. I've always had a few favourite bhangra tunes as well, so these also got me onto the dance floor. The D.J. was great because he was mixing in some R&B, hip hop beats and some of the bhangra tunes. The atmosphere on the dance floor was electric, it was the best wedding ever!

I had a couple of days off after the wedding as I knew I needed time to recuperate. I still sent Ky to nursery and it was nice just to have a bit of time to myself. Then, Jaz and I started trying for a baby.

Work was fantastic, getting better and better all the time. I was now working a lot for the directors of the I.T. Department. I was reporting directly to one director in particular and working on lots of projects with many departments. This was a great position to be in. It didn't stop my wants and desires for another child at all though. I always see work as a way to live, I don't live to work. I've always been very clear minded since I started work when I was sixteen as a trainee cashier for a bank and I've built my way up to being a project manager, always aiming high and studying along the way. I'd managed to get where I wanted to be. I was happy and content with my career path, my only next step from here would have been senior project manager.

Being a fulltime working mum and a project manager in a role which was extremely taxing at times I was starting to feel very tired. I thought maybe there was something wrong with me. Having said that I'd always loved my sleep, so I thought maybe it was just that my body wasn't getting as much sleep as it needed. Just to be on the safe side though, as anaemia was in my family I decided to go to the doctor and just get the things checked over.

Everything was fine so that was good, and he suggested it was probably just down to the hustle and bustle of life that comes with being a fulltime working mum.

I was being pulled into more and more projects and we were still trying for a baby. It wasn't happening as quickly as it had previously with Luca and Ky when it had been immediate. This was starting to play on my mind a little bit. I was wondering if maybe I was getting to the age when it was not going to be as easy as it was before, as I was now almost forty.

We had great news though that Steven and Grace were expecting their first child. Steven told us the news in November 2015, a honeymoon baby for sure, it was lovely. Part of me thought well, I'll get pregnant soon and the babies will grow up together. I was delighted and over the moon for them.

As we came to 2016 after a lovely Christmas at my mum and dads with my brothers and their wives, we had a lovely quiet new year at home, which we have done every year now since Luca passed away. I feel that we will always do this at New year, just have a quiet one at home, just the three of us.

In March 2016 I turned forty and we went back to Gran Canaria and again thoroughly enjoyed it. It was definitely our. I was spoilt by everybody at work and at home and by friends. It was a beautiful milestone birthday. Jas and I have the same birthday, but this birthday was all about me because it was my fortieth. He is two years younger than me.

Although work was busy and I was in a good place working with the directors on important projects, that March I had been expecting a big bonus and a pay rise, however that did not happen. Not only was I disappointed but many of my colleagues were as well who had been expecting the same rewards for their hard work. It was disheartening to think that I'd got so far in my career and no one was getting pay rises, but there was no bonus to be had as the company wasn't doing as well as they should and this made me think about what I wanted to do. There were going to be no sudden changes that's for sure and I was told by my line manager that I could still get a pay rise to recognise my hard work. This was done via a kind of nomination scheme of certain colleagues that goes to a board. I knew my name was floating about and all the directors knew me so surely after pulling off some very hard projects that others were not able to do, then I was a person who surely they would reward. Sadly, this again did not happen and around June 2016 I started looking for another job. I certainly wasn't being valued so I thought I'd have a look to see what was out there, nothing too serious as I was not in a hurry to leave.

I came across a job that I thought it would be good just to get some interview practice I was invited for an interview. The company was in the finance sector an area I had wanted to get into. There was a Building Society Headquarters near where I lived and this is where I ultimately wanted to be working, but they had no positions at the moment, so I thought this was with another building society cold be a good start. The interview went really well, and the job was located straight down an 'A' road about thirty-five minutes from where we lived. So, the journey time would be a little bit shorter to where I was currently. I was offered the position and it was twenty percent more money than I was earning currently, and they were offering me a car allowance. Although it ticked many of the boxes that I was looking for, there was still some travel time, but actually it was not that bad. I decided to take it after discussing it with Jas, realising it could be a very good fit for me, and that as there was only a three month probation, even if I did get pregnant within that time it would be fine, or we could even just wait until the new year before we tried again.

During this time, we had also had some checks done to make sure that we were still able to have baby. Everything had come back fine although it was slightly high on my thyroid check. Even though I was still within the normal range because being on the higher side of that can sometimes stop you from conceiving, the specialist that we saw had put me on levothyroxine to help with that.

I handed my notice in at the end of August 2016. I still had some annual leave I could take which shortened the amount of my notice. They were sad to see me go but unfortunately they could not match the salary that I was being offered so ultimately I had to leave. I was given a really good send of and initially kept in touch with some of the people I was working with, but as often happens with these things we ended up losing touch eventually.

In between starting the new job, I did a particularly good detox with Forever Living C9. It was brilliant. I lost seven pounds within nine days which was a very good start and I was feeling in a good place to continue trying for baby. That September I also added Luca to our surname so that his name would live on forever through us. At first it was just on Ky's and mine. Jas wasn't sure but he did eventually do it too. I started the new job with Luca in my surname which was a lovely feeling. However, when starting a new job, people want to get to know you and some asked if I was Italian. I explained that Luca was actually my first son who was stillborn, and we've added his name to our surname so that it lives on with us and sounds like a promise him. They found that to be so lovely and touching and a really nice way to remember Luca. For me it was hard to keep having to tell the same story.

Eventually I started to feel a little bit of anxiety every time I was asked, so to help me the doctor gave me a very low dosage of antidepressants just to get me back wo where I needed. I knew I wouldn't be with them for long, but like starting any new job it was daunting, so there was a little bit of pressure there.

A couple of weeks later I had a glowing review for my first month in the job and I realised that I actually didn't really need the antidepressants at all, everything was fine, and things had settled down. So, I thought I could just bring myself off them sooner and then tell the doctor which is what I started to do. I made an appointment to see the doctor as soon as I could.

I was really enjoying the new job; it had come given me a new set of challenges but that is always something I'm up for. I've always been career motivated and liked a challenge. I was also really enjoying the project that I'd been assigned and the people I was working with within this group were fantastic, we had a great rapport.

At the end of November on my way to work whilst stationary at a roundabout I was hit by a car from behind. The driver was a young woman who'd been on her mobile phone. She had have hit my SUV a Volkswagen Tiguan at the time with her small Corsa. It had jolted me forward in the car. It had not jolted the car however it did cause damage to the bumper underneath the plastic cover which had to be repaired although at the point of the crash, I couldn't see that it was damaged. When I got out of the car she was quite abrupt and shouting that there was no damage to my car and that everything was fine. I said that I needed to take her details nonetheless in case it isn't all fine. She didn't like this, and I also took a picture of her number plate just in case she'd given me false details. As I arrived late at work, I apologised to my manager and explained what had happened. One of my colleagues who was next to the manager could see that I was a bit shaken and took me to the canteen and made me a sweet mug of tea.

Later that afternoon I started to get a bit of pain in my neck and my manager said I should go home just in case it became whiplash and to make an appointment to see your doctor tomorrow if it starts to get any worse. Whilst at work I did phone my insurance company and let them know that I had been involved in an accident that morning. I gave the details of the girl who had gone into the back of my car. They arranged for my car to be seen at a Volkswagen registered body shop. It was then that we found out that the bumper was damaged underneath and needed to be repaired. The following day I was definitely in a lot of pain. It started coming on during the night. I was awfully bad by the next day and the doctor confirmed I had whiplash and gave me some medication. Following this I was unable to go into work. I was still within my three month probation period so wouldn't have got paid if I had gone off sick. As the project hadn't fully taken off yet, it was easy for me to do light work at home. I attended to my emails and nothing much more than that. So, I was able to rest and still send Ky to nursery. This went on until the new year.

That Christmas I was in a lot of pain and could hardly move. I'd thought the whiplash would be gone or at least have eased up by the time Christmas came but it didn't seem to be going anywhere. I did struggle not being able to do as much for Ky as I would normally have. The week in between the Christmas and New Year I became very poorly with a full on cold and fever. I felt awful. We had arranged to meet up with friends. These were friends I've mentioned earlier in the book, Rosie and Jassi and their husbands and children. We were due to meet at Rosie's house. Their husbands were friends of Jas from his school and college days. I'd met these ladies through our husbands, and we'd become extremely good friends, best friends, like sisters really. Our children were all similar ages, sort of a year or two between each of them and they had also become friends growing up together. As I was unwell Jas went with Ky and they had a great time. I stayed on the sofa and binge watched Suits on Netflix. I rested and drank lots of fluids and slept in between whenever I needed to. Before we knew it, the New Year was here. We had a quiet one at home as we normally do and then a few days later I went to work for the first time since the accident.

I was in horrific pain travelling to work which was now over an hour away each way because the company had moved offices in November. This made me realise I couldn't carry on like this and I needed to seek extra help from a physiotherapist. Seeing how I was struggling, my manager advised me to get an appointment with the physiotherapist as soon as I could. She told me I could do a couple of days at home. As the project still wasn't at full throttle, it was okay for me to work at home. But I needed to be in the office at least twice a week. So, we decided which days I would do in the office and which days I would do at home. We stuck to that for the next couple of months and I started seeing a physiotherapist. It was extremely hard to be travelling but it was something I had to do for my job. The pain was becoming more widespread now. It wasn't just in my neck and shoulders. It was also in my back, my hips and at the top of my legs, sometimes it would also go down my arms too. The headaches I was getting with it were horrific at times and all I wanted to do was lay down. I couldn't believe a small accident had caused so much pain. Jas suggested we book a holiday and go away. Maybe it would do me some good to getaway into some heat rather than the coldness we had here. So, we booked our favourite place again. We went to Gran Canaria and Jas was right, the heat did me good but then when I came back to the cold, I was back at square one again.

The project was ramping up and my manager needed me in the office a lot more on my return from the holiday. So, we had to decide what we were going to do. I was in so much pain that I was actually in tears after a meeting. I was so upset that it actually led to me having a mini breakdown at the office which wasn't great, but I was in a little side office by myself when this happened. I had to message one of my friends to come in to get me some tissues. When she saw how I was, she said this isn't right, you can't carry on like this, you need some help. It didn't really help that my manager had said that I didn't look depressed when I'd said to her that I had depression. Due to the pain, I hadn't ended up coming off the antidepressants because the whiplash started. The pain was getting so bad now that it didn't even cross my mind to come off them, so I was still taking them. I always went to work with makeup on. Having her say that I didn't look depressed wasn't really what I needed to hear then. I was in so much pain all over my body. Her saying that did tip me over and made me start crying, but mainly I was crying because of all the pain and pressure. I needed to do more at work. I couldn't understand how I was going to do that and travel into the office which was causing me more and more pain every time I travelled.

My friend suggested I talked to the Head of the Department who was my manager's manager and see what she thought. It took several attempts in the side office trying to get myself back together, then my friend went and called the Head of the Department. It took a while though because she was in a meeting but when she did come in and saw how I was, she asked me what had happened. I explained to her that I was in so much pain and I couldn't see how I was going to come into the office more because it was causing me even more pain to travel. She suggested that there was something more serious and that obviously my depression had got worse with all the pain. She suggested that I take some time out and go off sick and get myself checked out properly without having to worry about travelling or the project or anything else. She said the company would support me for as long as it takes and told me to take it month by month and do whatever I needed to get myself better.

I already had an appointment with my GP the following day because I needed to get some more painkillers. He also signed me off sick. He didn't increase my antidepressant medicine because he wanted to see how I got on that first month without any increase and see if anything improved. So, I had a month off and it slowly started to get warmer here in Warwickshire, but I wasn't getting any better in terms of pain. It wasn't getting any worse because I wasn't travelling anymore but it was sad that it wasn't getting any better either at this point. I was starting to see different doctors through the solicitors that my insurance company had appointed after the accident. It was starting to become clear this pain was still related to the accident but that it was no longer whiplash it was something else. My depression was getting worse and the pain was not easy so one of the doctors suggested that I see a chiropractor. My solicitors appointed a chiropractor and within a few sessions of seeing her she could tell that there was something wrong with my neck. She thought it might be a bulging disc and the only way to find this out would be by having a scan. After a few more sessions she wrote to my G.P. and suggested he referred me for an MRI.

Thankfully, the company were still paying me. I was in regular contact with Human Resources and they said that I had Bupa cover and gave me a number to contact to arrange to get an appointment at a private hospital. This had now taken us up to

August, so I'd been off now for five months. Within a space of three weeks, I saw the rheumatologist, had my MRI and I was diagnosed with arthritis of my neck, a bulging disc and fibromyalgia, a chronic pain disease which comes on with trauma such as a car accident. Fibro as it is known for in short, affects the whole body, so it made sense now as to why my whole body was always in pain and why I was so tired, because it also brings on fatigue. Once I had this diagnosis, Jas felt quite guilty for calling me lazy a few months before as all I ever wanted to do was sleep. This explained the fatigue but as there is no cure for this, I was told the only thing that I can do was to learn to manage it. I was referred to a pain management clinic and for CBT therapy to help me come to terms with my diagnosis and understand how to live within my limitations which would eventually become more and more evident. I was also put on more medication to help me manage the pain and as the cold months set in that eventually started getting worse.

Christmas again was full of pain as it has been every year since but now I needed to learn how to manage my new way of life. How strange it was that I had to learn a new way of life yet again, first when Luca had died and now with this chronic illness that had I been diagnosed with. Inside I felt defeated I couldn't understand what was coming of my life. I still couldn't return to work because the pain was too intense. It was the year we had the Beast from the East and one of the worst winters we'd had for a long time.

Ky started school in the September before. He was in Reception Class, so my days were spent wrestling sometimes with so many medications that it was quite difficult to focus. Sometimes I'd be out of it and I would sleep during the day. I had to set my alarm to go and pick up Ky from school. I couldn't quite understand how my life had come to this from being somebody who was active before the accident, doing yoga, boxercise and spinning classes, and now I was not able to do anything.

Christmas and New Year came and went. That January Ky was five and a half and he asked me how Luca had died. I knew one day this question would come and I'd known it would be quite soon, still it took me by surprise. It came out of the blue; we hadn't even been talking about him. We were just watching television and suddenly he asked. This is where the idea for the childrens book 'Why did Grandad Die?' was born. I realise this is such a difficult conversation to have with a child and therefore needed to make it available with profits to go to The Luca Foundation.

I was no longer being paid but I was still employed. I was just trying to find a way to get back to work this year. My employer and I looked at different ways of how to get me working from home. Being a fulltime project manager that was not ideal. Plus, with the brain fog I would get with the fibromyalgia I wasn't sure I wanted to go straight back into a fulltime project management role, I needed something to ease me in. So, we looked at the office near me at the other end of the M69. There was an office in Leicester which would be nearer for me to get to and not be such a long drive, but unfortunately there were no jobs that I could do there, not even part-time. After a few meetings it became clear that I would not be able to return to work and I was let go of on the basis of poor health.

This was four days before my birthday and Jas's fortieth, not a fantastic start to that week. I had saved up a lot of the money however from when I was being paid during the first six months that I was off. We had decided to go to for Dubai five nights which was lovely. My parents had gone to do a tour of India and Korea and on their way back they were stopping off in Dubai, so they were there for a couple of nights and we were able to do somethings together. They enjoyed being able to have a day out with Ky which is something that they'd never done really before. We all went to the underwater zoo at the Dubai mall on the day of our birthdays and then after that my parents left us to enjoy the rest of our day as the three of us.

We had a fantastic holiday in Dubai and realised that five nights was not enough because there was so much to do as that had opened theme parks as well. We will go back one day for sure.

Summary

As you can tell, having another child no matter what other people say, does not and never will take the pain away of losing your child. It definitely does not replace your other child either. What it does do though, is give you somewhere else to focus your attention on and that itself helps towards building your life again, whilst you still carry the grief with you.

I have found over the years that grief is like an inflatable backpack. Sometimes, it is full and heavy with grief, other times less so, however it is always there and never goes away. Of course, it never will either, not when you have lost your own flesh and blood, the baby you loved from the moment you had pregnant come up on your test. You grieve for them and all the plans and life you should have had with them too. To me it is mother nature gone wrong.

We have always kept Luca's photos up in the house, and kept him part of all our special days, Mother's Day, Father's Day, birthdays, and Christmas. We have always cut a cake on his birthday, just the three of us and then sent a balloon that we have all kissed up to heaven.

I feel for children that have lost a parent at a young age too. Parents are meant to be here to help nurture their child well into full adulthood and see their grandchildren be born.

Now when I hear of someone passing aged eighty or above, I think, I'm glad they lived a full life. As sad as it is that they have gone and will be dearly missed, I now think wow how much they must have got to see. 'Why did Grandad Die?' can be purchased at www.thelucafoundation.org.uk

Chapter 5
Growing Pains

After Easter I developed sciatica. This is a symptom of fibro and something I've never had before. The pain was awful, it made me cry. I couldn't walk properly and needed a walking stick. This continued for many weeks into June and over Ky's birthday. It was also the time of Luca's 6th anniversary and for the first time on this occasion I was by myself.

Ky was at school and Jas was at work. There was no need to have those two weeks off anymore because Ky was at school and instead we would go on holiday during the summer school break. Luca's birthday hit me like a tsunami. I wasn't expecting this it came out of nowhere. There were many reasons for this, not just that it was the anniversary of Luca's death but also that I was crippled with pain, had lost my career, and didn't know what my future held. I was still getting used to managing my illness.

All of the issues that this illness had caused me and then it being Luca's anniversary was just too much and it caused a complete and utter breakdown. I sobbed and cried and screamed into pillows, it was uncontrollable. It was as if Luca had just died again and the pain was so fresh. All this crying, sadness and heartbreak put me into what is called fibre flare.

This is when your body becomes so exhausted that you take to your bed. This continued for the next three days.

On the actual day I was in no state to be able to pick Ky up from school, so I asked my friend whose daughter is in the same class if she could drop Ky off home. She knew exactly why and when she did I dropped to my knees at the front door and flung my arms around Ky. He was exactly what I needed that day. My friend said that he was exactly what I'd been waiting for all day, and I agreed. She could read me like a book but I suppose any mother would be able to understand that moment whilst you're grieving for one child and all you really want to do is wrap your arms around your other child too, or several children as it may be for some.

We had stopped trying for another baby once the accident had happened and I was in excruciating pain. After the week of Ky birthday and Luca's anniversary and birthday, somehow with having the sciatica, I twisted the knee of my right leg. I didn't feel it immediately as I was already feeling so much pain from the sciatica, which was going down my leg too. I now always walked with a walking stick. It wasn't until my knee swelled up like a balloon that I knew something was wrong. I found this out in the last week of June/ early July when I had an appointment with the pain management clinic. They said it could be fibromyalgia but if it doesn't calm down in a couple of weeks go see you G.P. I did exactly that as it wasn't calming down and it was a really hot summer and all my other aches and pains how become a lot easier to deal with. The sciatica had subsided, but my knee was still extremely painful and swollen. I saw my GP around the end of July, and he said that he would refer me for an MRI scan.

Before I had twisted my knee, we had booked to go back to Gran Canaria for the last week of August before school started again. I wasn't quite sure how I was going to manage with my knee being so bad but there's no way we could cancel, and the MRI wasn't actually going to happen until early September after the holiday. I struggled but I bought a nice strap to help me with my walking. As I had a walking stick at the airport they helped me jump the queues so that I could then sit down as soon as I could. On the holiday it felt like we were having two separate holidays, Jas and Ky would go off during the day to the beach or into the town and to the parks etc I would just lie on the sunbeds near the pool of the apartment suites. As we had been a few times to the same place it was actually quite easy for us to plan out what we were doing. It was all level, so it wasn't going to be as hard for me walking and everything was nearby. I would walk to a restaurant in the evening but everything else was at the apartment complex. Jas and Ky would join me at the poolside after they've had their day out. I felt like I was missing out on having a good holiday with Ky, but he was having a lot of fun with his dad. It is what it is I thought, I will just make the most of what I can do even though this wasn't much. Nonetheless it was nice to be away and I had time to completely relax. I was hoping if I went in the pool it may help my knee, but it didn't.

I had my MRI when we returned back home. Ky went back to school and Jas was back at work. It took three to four weeks to get my results. I was still continuously in pain and didn't know what was wrong with my knee, but I knew it wasn't the fibro. The pain with fibro is quite different to what was happening with my knee. Anybody that's ever had a twisted knee which turned out to be a grade two sprain will know how painful it is. Fibro pain is all over the body, a dull nagging pain that never goes away. Some days it's easier than others but nonetheless it's always there. After getting my results the doctor said it would probably be best to do a cortisone injection however this was going to be administered at the doctor's surgery by a GP that was trained to do it.

At the end of October during half term week, I was to have my steroid injection and Jas had taken part of that week off, so the timing fell right. Lots of people told me it would be fine, and you won't really feel it. All three of us went. Jas needed to go with me so he could drive me home and there was no one for us to leave Ky with. What a mistake that was! The injection was extremely painful it was like having an epidural during giving birth and I screamed. The doctor said she's never had anybody scream like that when having a steroid injection and realised it would be the fibromyalgia that was making me hypersensitive to it. In the past needles never bothered me but I'd become hypersensitive to needles because of the fibro. Ky got scared because I was screaming, and this is where I felt extremely guilty that he was there. I reassured him that I was okay even though I had tears in my eyes. Needless to say, when we were back home he was constantly asking me if I was okay. My poor baby had to see his mommy going through that. Inside I was cursing those people that had told me it was okay, and I wouldn't feel anything when it had been completely the opposite.

The pain actually got worse after the steroid injection. I ended up in bed for quite a number of days, so I missed out on half term with Ky. Luckily, Jas was off, so they were able to do things together. Yet again another holiday with him being off school that I was missing out on doing things with him. A few weeks after I had to have a check-up with my GP I was trying to walk without my walking stick and it was okay to do short distances, but I wasn't able to do go further for example to go around the shops. In August I was given a blue badge because I was unable to walk very well at all. I was also having physio to get my anterior cruciate ligament strong again and overall make the knee stronger. For some reason this aggravated the knee. We didn't really know why. I was in such agony with the knee and the fibromyalgia as it was winter again and every single part of my body was in so much pain. I cried on Jas's shoulder and said I can't continue like this. We decided to see a private chiropractor. I went to one that had been recommended by a few people who had seen her. I got an appointment as soon as I could. It turned out that the kneecap had somehow moved out of place and she was going to have to slowly move it back. Because of the fibro it couldn't be done all in one go so she could only do a fifth of the amount of work on me than she would do on a normal healthy person. There had to be quite a number of sessions. It turns out that my hip was not aligned which was also causing a problem down my leg and I was putting more pressure on my knee. She explained that if my foot was on the brake at the time of the accident, this would have caused my hip alignment to be moved, which then had a the knock on effect on that side. It's always my right side. The sciatica was on my right side, my twisted knee was the right leg, not to mention all the back pain, neck pain and shoulder pain. I was a walking bag of pain.

After a couple of months, I was in a better state. It started getting warm again which was great. Jas suggested we take a holiday again to Gran Canaria. This was the place where I knew I could relax and they had lots to do, and the warm weather would do me good. So, over the Easter Holidays 2019, we went for a short holiday to Gran Canaria. The weather did do me good and it was great to be out in the warm weather end again, although I couldn't do much because I was still walking with a stick. Sitting on a plane wasn't overly comfortable but it was only a four-hour flight. I was able to adjust my position quite a number of times to get myself comfortable. My main aim through the flight was to get some rest and then I wanted to get some warmth on my bones. This was the last holiday that we ended up having.

Ky wanted to go back to Disneyland Paris again as we had for his third and fourth birthday way before the problems with my sciatica and knee started. We explained that there was no way mummy could walk around Disneyland and that we would go once I was better. We were nearly a year on now, since the knee problem and my chiropractor suggested that there was probably something more going on. She said I needed to have an MRI scan again. So, we went through the same process again with the GP referring me I had an MRI at a private hospital. They found that I had cartilage damage, but the knee structure itself was fine. It was the fibro that was actually causing so much pain there. I recently found out that as fibromyalgia is such a complex illness, if you are severely injured like I was with my knee, the brain signals to that area will keep it in constant pain.

There is no cure, no operation that can stop this. After seeing three consultants the diagnosis I had, was that there was never going to be a cure for my knee and that I would probably never be able to walk properly again. The only thing they could try which I'm still waiting for to this day, is to have three of the six nerves in my knee blocked with nerve block. This would then send signals to my brain to lessen the pain. Hopefully, I would then be able to exercise my knee and strengthen it to the point where I could start walking again. This is an extremely long process and there's no guarantee that it would even work. So, I now have to accept that I am a person with limitations. I have to focus on what I can do with the strength that I do have, which is not very much unfortunately. So, having a normal life and being able to kick around a football with my son like I used to before all this happened is looking extremely unlikely, but I never lose hope. I've always been an optimistic person and always try to look for the silver lining although at times it's really hard to find that silver lining. I know I have to keep going as my little young man is watching me, his mother, who's poorly with limitations, but a fighter that keeps going on.

Alicia Keys, song 'Superwoman' is played even more in my life now. Originally this song helped me when Luca died, where I could find no silver lining. That's definitely one area of my life from which there can be no silver lining. The words of this song spoke out to me, as many of Alicia Keys' songs do. It touches you in many ways, it makes you realise how it plays a part in your life. I find that music does this quite a lot and certain artists do that for me.

For example, when I split up with my first husband, Destiny's Child's song 'Survivor' was released. Lots of things were said to me by my family, but it was that Survivor song that gave me the strength to stand up and say I'll show you I am a survivor and will do better. I will have a good life; you have not taken that away from me. The words of Jameila's song 'Thank You', were also very fitting at that time. "Thank you for every last bruise you gave me, every time I sat in tears, as I wouldn't be enjoying my life now." That always made me smile. I had no regrets and really started to live a life of enjoyment with friends and family.

The 'Superwoman' words,

I am a superwoman, yes I am, yes she is,
Even when I'm a mess,
I still put on a vest,
with an S on my chest, oh yes, I'm a superwoman.

When I'm breaking down,
and I can't be found,
And I start to get weak,
Cause no one knows'

me underneath these clothes,
But I can Fly,
We can Fly, ooh

I am a Superwoman,
Yes I am,
Yes she is,
Even when I'm a mess,
I put on a vest,
with an S on my chest,
oh yes,
cos I'm a superwoman.

So now I'll take you back to the time of my breakdown on Luca's 6th anniversary in June 2018. That actually became my breakthrough. What that did was make me the superwoman this song talks about. It made me want to start a charity in Luca's memory. That charity would give a cuddle cot to all maternity units across the UK to ensure that bereaved parents in baby loss, don't go through what we did when we didn't have that cuddle cot. What the cuddle cot does, is give the gift of time. Time that you will never have again with your little baby before you have to say your goodbyes to then never see them again.

I launched the charity, called The Luca Foundation in November 2018. With the help of lots of fundraisers and supporters we raised over £8,500 in our first nine months. I was also nominated as an inspirational person of the year for the Midlands Business and Community Charity Awards. This was a huge, lovely surprise for me. It meant that people recognised that I was doing something good out of my grief for others, but also I was doing this whilst suffering with the chronic illness of fibromyalgia.

2019 ended on a high for me. I'd accomplished so much with the charity and found my inner strength to manage my illness. It was still extremely hard at times and I was still having very bad days quite often. I would try not to let it get me down and I worked through those hard times. I had also started writing this book and a children's book based on the conversation that I had with Ky about how Luca died, when Ky was five years old in January 2018.

When 2020 arrived, I was full of hope, ambition and excited about the year ahead. I had decided that I would name my book Angel Warrior which is my new name for bereaved parents and the name I hope catches on and its approved by bereaved parents. It's nicer and easier to say I'm an Angel Warrior. So, I decided that I also wanted to have a tee shirt or hoodie that has the symbol of Angel Warrior on it and the words as well as a little logo. I wanted this to be complementary to the book, but also so that parents that are bereaved can wear it, and the name would catch on and people would know they have lost a child. It's an easier way and form of saying that. This made me think of a few more other things that I could put on clothing that would be easier to wear rather than say. Suddenly, I had so many mental health slogans in my head I had to write them all down. This gave me the idea of launching my own clothing line, but this needed a lot of research and guidance. I have sought this from the Chambers of Commerce near me who provide free support for those that want to start the business. I had the idea at the end of January, and I started looking into what I needed to do. One thing I wanted is for it to be future friendly, earth friendly, environmentally friendly, vegan friendly so I decided eco-friendly clothing was what I wanted to do. I want to have lots of mental health slogans and for part of the profits to support other charities like the Samaritans, NSPCC, war veterans and sports charities, the Luca Foundation of course and an anti-knife crime charity. Eco-friendly clothing not only helps the earth, but its animal friendly with no toxins or chemicals in the clothing and its sustainable fashion. Now in thinking about the slogan, I've realised that it's probably a slogan that people are going to wear for many years. If you're very passionate about it like I am, then I would wear them all year round whether that be a T-shirt, a sweatshirt or hoodie.

It was also now time for me to get my own independence back. I had worked since I was sixteen but then having lost my career to the fibro, I was now without any income. I was relying on my husband and I absolutely hated asking for money. I had always been an independent woman and I wanted to gain that back. I don't take any money out of the charity to pay myself, and we have no overheads as I run it from home and none of the trustees are paid. The only thing that is ever paid out is any expenses that are needed for the charity, such as collection envelopes. This book and my clothing line will be my only source of income and help me to regain some of my independence back. Even a small percentage of the profits from this book will go to The Luca Foundation so that we can support more maternity units across the UK to ensure that they have working cuddle cots available as soon as the traumatic thing happens to a family, where they suffer baby loss.

I was very limited as to what I could do, but I knew what I was doing was within my limits. The books once they are written and published do not really take much of my time anymore. For the clothing business I have somebody doing the heavy lifting and hard work of printing them for me. I then just need to pack them and post them to my customers. Jas can then take them to the post office when he comes back from work. A lot of thought and preparation has gone into things, especially when I have to work it around my illness. If I do have a few bad days while I am in bed, I know that I can rely on my subcontractor and on Jas to pick up the parts that I cannot do. I hope and pray that these bad days are very few and far between and that I can manage this more by myself.

I decided that the business will be for all age groups, male and female. I support lots of campaigns including Black Lives Matter, Pride, the Heads Up Campaign which encourages men to speak out about mental health, and many more.

Then coronavirus hit. At one point, I thought there was going to be no way I could start nor finish these projects. Then Jas was furloughed from his job for a large car manufacturer who he worked for in Coventry, not far from where we live in Warwickshire. This meant that I was able to apply for funding from the council and charitable organisations to produce the children's book. We then decided after talking to the charities commission that we could ask for businesses to sponsor the book and their information to be added to the book, as a thank you for their funds towards the project. So, in April I spent a lot of time filling in funding applications. Then by late May we had funds coming in to start phase one of the project which was the illustrations.

In late May my parents decided to loan me the money I needed to start my business and produce this book, so that I could regain control of my life, as they had seen me struggle for over three years now. They loved my business idea and knew it would be a great way for them to support me. My mum knows I have always been a giver and was so pleased that I would also be supporting other charities through my business. I believe that if all business did this, the world would be a better place.

During my research I found that eco-friendly clothing was generally quite expensive to buy. So, I looked long and hard for a good UK based supplier so that I could meet customer demand as the business grew. What I knew was that I would not be charging the exceedingly high prices that many other eco-friendly clothing companies do. I ordered samples and we as a family wore them, washed them, and checked for the durability of the fabric. All my boxes were being ticked. Now I knew we could go ahead. For us there was good coming out of the lockdown. I was able to put all my time into my work with the added bonus of Jas being home to look after Ky. We shared the home-schooling and Jas did the grocery shopping once a week. We had our masks and hand gel everywhere, ready to use immediately.

The only time I went out was when my chiropractor could see me. The first two months were complete agony for me, until they reopened. I also went to local shops for meat and fresh fruit and vegetables.

Mother's Day, our ten-year wedding anniversary and Ky's seventh birthday were all done in lockdown. We made the most of all the nice weather and we even got tans as though we had been on holiday. We counted our blessings that we had a garden we could enjoy and a pool to put out for Ky on the hot days, as well of course each other. We did family quiz nights on zoom and I did good old girlie catch up with my girlfriends on WhatsApp video calls too. We have been thanking God for all this great technology. VE day celebrations were small, but we marked this important date nonetheless. I caught up with my only remaining grandparent every week to check she was ok. She lives in Leicester and I could not go, but my Uncle Pat lived nearby and did shopping for her. Things could have been a lot worse, but I was looking on the bright side as much as I can, whenever I can. I felt blessed and started doing a gratitude diary with Ky for the things we are grateful to have. Yes, like most couples, Jas and I had plenty of arguments during lockdown too.

Over these few months during lockdown I was very much as Alicia Keys would say "This girl is on fire!" I had completed both my books this one and the children's book, along with launching my eco-friendly clothing line in the summer of 2020.

Final Summary

Between 2018 and the summer of 2020, I have learned a lot about myself. I found the strength to be the superwoman I needed to be, not just for myself, but for my young son, for my husband and for us as a family as I continued to keep Luca's memory alive. I had to find a new way of living again as I was limited in what I could do both physically and mentally. I found that pretending to be okay was exhausting. Pretending to be someone that you're not with fibro and always saying yes I'm fine when people ask how you are is very tiring. I was not always fine and many times I wanted to say no I'm struggling big time, however what was that person actually going to do to help me? Mentally yes it would have been better to get it off my chest and say to somebody I wasn't fine.

I would have nightmares during this time.. nightmares where I would be yelling at complete strangers looking at me bizarrely because of my limitations and how I was doing mentally. I would be shouting at them, 'I'm not well, I am not a well person.' I think my subconscious was trying to tell me that was locked into the body of somebody that I didn't want to be. I wanted to scream and shout at people and to say, this is not who I want to be, this is not me, I'm unwell, and I can't help it. I think a lot of my frustrations have been played out in my dreams. The frustrations of people not understanding fibromyalgia and also the frustration I had with myself in living the life I was living.

This was all down to the fibromyalgia. It had stopped me from having a third child, it ended my career, it had changed our lives beyond recognition and that was a hard blow to take. The only thing I could do now was really focus on my abilities, although I would get confused and mixed up with my words and this is also due to the cognitive behaviour of the brain when you have fibro.

I was also finding that my pain was now in my hands and my feet. So, whilst doing this book, I was dictating it, rather than typing it as writing it which would hurt my hands. My feet would ache even when I was laying down. Jas would quite often have to wake up and massage my feet as I wasn't able to sleep, but once he did it I would be able to sleep along with this. I was experiencing a lot of restless nights and a lot of my symptoms were getting worse. I was determined however that I was going to write this book, to help many of you out there who are Angel Warriors. I felt it was also important as it would help those who are supporting Angel Warriors.

I think it's fair to say that lots of things that have happened in my life. When I was eleven, my first cousin was diagnosed with leukaemia. She was eleven months younger than me. I watched for a year as she battled the illness. There was one stage where she looked so well as if she was recovering, but a year later in June, I was twelve and she was eleven and she deteriorated and sadly we lost her. She was my first cousin, my sister, my best friend, the one that I would always hang out with in the school holidays and we were always together at every opportunity. I didn't like family get-togethers after that because she wasn't there, I didn't really want to hang out with the rest of my cousins because they were also much younger. At the age of sixteen, my dad's youngest brother married his lovely wife and finally I started to enjoy family get-togethers again, as I really enjoyed her company and still do to this day.

When I was fourteen, I was involved in a school bus crash. I went to school in Loughborough, a have couple of towns away from where I lived. It was a bad crash, many of us were thrown from the bus and some of the children and the driver went into intensive care. This was all because a lorry was overtaking on a blind bend and smacked into the side of the bus, sending us into a ditch.

At the age of sixteen I lost my first grandparent, my mum's father, my Papa. He had a heart attack on his way home from work at the mere age of fifty-eight. It was hard to see my mum grieving so heavily, but I stepped up. I was working full time as a trainee cashier in the bank and I looked after my younger brothers. I did the cooking at home as well.

Then at the age of twenty two, I had this arranged marriage to a guy who pretended to be something he wasn't during our engagement. I ended up in an abusive marriage, physically, mentally, emotionally but with the support of my family I was able to get out of it. That was the best decision I've ever made.

Having all these things happen at an early age which were never recognised in those days, means that I can now relate to something I read in Frankie Bridges book recently which is called 'Open.' I now realise that I developed an anxiety disorder. Doctors didn't recognise this at those times in the 1980's and 1990's. I would sometimes say that I was suffering with headaches and stomach aches. These are the first signs now that we look for in children with anxiety problems.

Luckily, I was the type of person that found the strength within myself and throughout everything I've gone through in my life I've come through it, in the best way I could. Losing Luca however was the one time I never thought I would come through. A time when I thought of taking my own life. Somehow however with the grace of God, that darkness of a desire to take my own life disappeared. Losing your child is the absolute worst and darkest thing you could ever go through and I'm sure anybody could imagine that. It is the worst type of loss and changes you forever.

Eventually I found the strength to carry on and have our second son and get back to work and start living a life again, enjoying life again. I planned to have another child with my husband Jas. I was fit and active, doing boxercise, yoga, and spinning classes. I was running around with my little boy, playing football, basketball, hide and seek, all the fun things you play with your little child.

Little did we know that our lives would take another drastic change. This was due to some young girl being on her phone whilst driving, not paying full attention, and going into the back of my car. She jolted me forward in my chair, whilst I was looking to the right and caused so many problems within my body which then resulted in a chronic illness called Fibromyalgia.

This eventually changed our lives beyond recognition. My son now seven doesn't remember the days when I used to play football with him in the garden, take him to the park do all those fun things that an active mum can do. His childhood memories of me now will be either sleeping or in too much pain to do anything. Hopefully over time, he'll remember that I gave it my all to do as much as I could for him. He is the reason that I live now. He is the reason that I'm doing what I do. He was the inspiration for the children's book because of the conversation that we had. This has now transpired into a book to help other children understand bereavement. He is the one that gives me the strength to write this book and explain my journey as a bereaved parent.

Whilst my husband has now been the sole supporter of our family, for the last three and a half years, it is now time for me to do something to give me a little independence. I had to think long and about I could do with the disabilities I live with now, knowing that my knee will never be fully recovered. If the nerve block is successful, I know that I'm going to have to have that regularly, just to be able to keep me walking and moving a small amount. If it is unsuccessful however, then I know that in setting up my clothing line I have people around me that can help. I'm determined to be able to do it by myself and let's face it, all I'm really doing is printing off labels, packaging the garments and Jas will then post them out.

Yes of course there will be times when I'm struggling a lot. Times I will be stuck in bed. Times where I have no energy to do anything, but unfortunately that's the reality of my life now. I have to accept this illness. I could be a person that sits back and gives into it all and doesn't live a life or even try to live a life, but I'm not that kind of person as you can tell. From the age of twelve having lost my cousin I still fought back. After going through an abusive marriage, I came back stronger than ever. I still somehow came back from having lost my child, and that just shows that I'm a fighter, I'm a warrior. I'm an Angel Warrior and that is a hard life to live, but I live it, nonetheless. It's become harder to live obviously with having fibro, there are so many more challenging times in these circumstances.

The way I see it is that when Ky grows up and understands what his mum has gone through, he'll understand that you always have to show your strength and courage to get through the hard times in life.

He will see that his mum has been a fighter and will always be a fighter who tries not to give in. Sometimes I have given in and at these times, he sees me in bed for days on end and the day out that I planned has to cancelled at the last minute. I say sorry, we can't go now, mummy is not well again. One day he'll understand that I did as much as I could. On days I just couldn't, they break my heart, having to cancel things he Is looking forward to because of my chronic illness.

As a mother I always thought I'd be able to give the best to be my children. I worked to build up my career to do just that. To have all that taken away because of somebody else is hard to contemplate and at times I get angry about it. Now though I'm at a stage where even though I still do get angry about it, I'm doing the best that I can. I'm going to build this business up and help for other charities as well as my own. I will help people wear a mental health slogan even if it's hard for them to say it themselves.

I'm going to run The Luca Foundation in memory of Luca and support other bereaved parents and families in the most traumatic circumstances, by ensuring that all maternity units across the UK have working cuddle cots. If over time we as a charity can do more, then we will certainly do that.

So I ask you the reader to help us at The Luca Foundation to support families who are going through and have gone through what I have in this book, so that they can make memories with the Angel Baby before their final goodbyes. Something I will always regret not having, but most importantly can now make available for others.

As I've mentioned before, myself and the other trustees do not get paid out of the charity. I am doing this from my own home, so we have no overheads to pay out. As it stands at this moment, if you are a person that prefers eco-friendly clothing, I ask you to support my clothing line LK Eco Style and as an Angel Warrior, please let's all together make Angel Warrior the new name for a bereaved parent. You can purchase your Angel Warrior top from LK eco style. This will help me to make a living for myself, so that I can continually do the work of the charity and hopefully more people will be helped through that.

MARCIA M
PUBLISHING HOUSE

www.marciampublishing.com

Printed in Great Britain
by Amazon